CDFI FUND
CAPACITY
BUILDING
INITIATIVE
Advancing. Innovating. Sustaining.

Searching for Markets:

The Geography of Inequitable Access to Healthy & Affordable Food in the United States

THE REINVESTMENT FUND
Capital at the point of impact.

The CDFI Fund invests in and builds the capacity of community-based, private, for-profit and non-profit financial institutions with a primary mission of community development in economically distressed communities. These institutions – certified by the CDFI Fund as community development financial institutions or CDFIs – are able to respond to gaps in local markets that traditional financial institutions are not adequately serving. CDFIs provide critically needed capital, credit and other financial products in addition to technical assistance to community residents and businesses, service providers, and developers working to meet community needs.

For more information about the CDFI Fund and its programs, please visit the Fund's website at: http://www.cdfifund.gov.

About the Community Development Financial Institutions Fund's Financing Healthy Food Options Track

The CDFI Fund is providing training and technical assistance to CDFIs that are engaged in, or wish to become engaged in, healthy food financing activities. The CDFI Fund is offering a series of training workshops focused on the key elements of financing healthy food projects. There will be a total of eight training sessions held throughout the country in 2011 and 2012, with three different healthy food finance tracks offered: 1) farms and food production; 2) mid-tier food chain enterprises (e.g., food aggregation; food processing; food distribution); and 3) food retailers. At each session, trainers with practical experience and expertise will lead participants to drill down into the specific fundraising, underwriting, and loan management skills required for successful healthy food projects in low-income communities.

CDFIs that complete the training are eligible to receive, at no cost, up to 40 hours of individual technical assistance from subject matter experts. In addition, the following free resources are available through the Capacity Building Initiative website to workshop attendees and non-attendees:

- National Demand for Healthy Food Options Report: A robust, in-depth study of areas with low access to healthy foods in low income communities across the country.

- Financial Resources Catalogue: Primary public and private sources of financing available to CDFIs to finance healthy foods initiatives.

- Training Curriculum: A series of original training curriculum that showcases best practices and case studies in successful healthy food financing.

- Food Desert Mapping Tools. Mapping tools designed to help practitioners understand where low food access areas exist in their communities.

OPPORTUNITY**FINANCE**
NETWORK

Opportunity Finance Network (OFN), the leading network of private financial institutions, creates growth that is good for communities, investors, individuals, and the economy. Members of OFN are community development financial institutions (CDFIs) that deliver responsible lending to help low-wealth and low-income communities join the economic mainstream. More information is available at: www.opportunityfinance.net.

 THE REINVESTMENT FUND
Capital at the point of impact.

TRF is a national leader in rebuilding America's distressed towns and cities and does this work through the innovative use of capital and information. TRF has invested $1 billion in mid-Atlantic communities since 1985. As a CDFI, TRF finances projects related to housing, community facilities, food access, commercial real estate, and energy efficiency. It also provides public-policy expertise by helping clients create practical solutions and by sharing data and analyses via PolicyMap. Beginning with the Pennsylvania Fresh Food Financing Initiative (FFFI) in 2004, TRF has developed a comprehensive approach to improving the food landscape in low-income, underserved communities. As principal manager of FFFI, TRF secured nearly $150 million in private and public capital to match a $30 million seed investment from the Commonwealth of Pennsylvania. Since then, TRF has financed 93 projects to increase access to healthy food across the state, with funds expended totaling over $100 million. These projects have created or retained more than 5,500 jobs and 1.85 million square feet of retail space for healthy food. TRF's financing successes have become the model for related projects in several states, as well as for the Obama administration's national Healthy Food Financing Initiative.

Letter from CDFI Fund

I am pleased to present a new research report focused on healthy food accessibility across the country. The Searching for Markets: *The Geography of Inequitable Access to Healthy & Affordable Food in the United States* report is the result of in-depth research and evaluation of "Limited Supermarket Access" areas, or LSAs. Over 24 million people live in these areas, eight percent of the total U.S. population, and as a result they must travel significantly farther to reach a supermarket than those living in communities with easier access to grocery stores.

This report was produced for the Community Development Financial Institutions Fund's (CDFI Fund) Capacity Building Initiative, which provides training and technical assistance to Community Development Financial Institutions (CDFIs) on current and emerging issues. Under the initiative a sub-series on Financing Healthy Food Options was offered. The Reinvestment Fund, as part of a contract with the Opportunity Finance Network (the series' lead contractor) designed the study to help investors and CDFIs identify areas with both inadequate access to healthy food and sufficient market demand for food retail across the United States.

The report provides important findings, such as the greater likelihood of LSA residents being low-income and of a minority race. These two groups have always been priorities for the CDFI Fund's programs, underscoring how all aspects of a community's development, from where its residents work and shop to wear they buy their groceries, are viable starting points for investments in struggling neighborhoods.

The report also serves as a valuable tool for CDFIs interested in healthy food lending opportunities in low-income communities, providing important information about LSA area market characteristics. It ties in handily with the other resources provided by the Financing Healthy Food Options series, available on the CDFI Fund's website. The CDFI Fund is committed to expanding the capacity of CDFIs engaged in healthy food lending in low-income communities. Whether it is through our competitive award programs or through the training and technical assistance offered under the Capacity Building Initiative, we are actively working to support CDFIs' healthy food lending efforts.

I hope this report provides yet more valuable information for CDFIs engaged in healthy food lending. For more information about the Capacity Building Initiative, and the CDFI Fund's other programs, please visit our website at www.cdfifund.gov.

Sincerely,

Donna J. Gambrell
Director, CDFI Fund

Table of Contents

List of Tables & Maps and Figures

Tables in Main Text

Tables in Appendix

Maps

Figures

Searching for Markets:
The Geography of Inequitable Access to Healthy & Affordable Food in the United States

Executive Summary

Financing the construction of new supermarkets and the expansion of existing stores has emerged as a strategy for increasing access to sources of healthy food. The Pennsylvania Fresh Food Financing Initiative (FFFI) used strategic financing as a mechanism for attracting supermarkets to distressed communities and for assisting small stores in expanding or upgrading their facilities throughout Pennsylvania. The FFFI program, which was managed by The Reinvestment Fund (TRF), serves as a model for Community Development Financial Institutions (CDFIs) seeking to establish and operate programs.

In an effort to help CDFIs build their capacity to finance healthy food options, the U.S. Department of the Treasury's Community Development Financial Institutions Fund (CDFI Fund) established the Financing Healthy Food Options track. This program, managed by Opportunity Finance Network (OFN), offers training, information and technical assistance and has provided funding for this Limited Supermarket Access (LSA) study. While several prior studies have sought to identify areas with inadequate access to food, sometimes referred to as food deserts, none were specifically designed to provide CDFIs with the necessary data to evaluate projects and prioritize investment areas.

This paper describes our LSA study, including our review of prior research methods, the methodological steps that comprised the LSA analysis and a summary of our findings. TRF's LSA methodology is unique in that, in addition to identifying areas, it provides descriptive information about market conditions, including figures that quantify the demand and unmet demand for food. Through this study, TRF seeks to assist decision-makers by providing them with data that shows high-priority areas for intervention in their target areas.

TRF's LSA analysis used recent U.S. census population data and 2011 industry-specific store-location data and combined this information with rigorous spatial and statistical methods to identify areas within the U.S. that have inequitable access to supermarkets. The LSA results are publicly available, allowing CDFIs to go beyond identifying problematic areas to providing descriptive information about each area to consider during the underwriting process. TRF's LSA study estimates the extent of the problem, including the unmet demand for food and the area's leakage (food dollars that residents spend outside of the area). These elements are essential for CFDIs seeking to determine appropriate interventions and to direct resources to viable projects.

CDFI Fund recognizes that public resources are always scarce and must be allocated to projects that provide the greatest public benefits, build from market opportunities and can last beyond the initial public-investment period. Thus this study seeks to highlight areas meeting these criteria. Some results are highlighted in this document, and further results are easily available to CDFIs, store operators and the general public for the entire continental U.S. through PolicyMap at policymap.com. PolicyMap is an online data and mapping tool provided by TRF that allows users to view data both spatially and in tabular form. PolicyMap has more than 15,000 data points and various tools for analyzing data spatially. Much of the data that PolicyMap provides, including the components of the LSA analysis and the store locations used in the analysis, are available at no charge to the public and can be viewed, downloaded and shared.

TRF's LSA study establishes benchmarks based on actual distances that households in well-served communities travel to stores and compares all communities around the country to these benchmarks. The benchmarks vary based on an area's population density and car-ownership rate. This methodology avoids a "one-size-fits-all" strategy by recognizing that households travel reasonable but varied distances to reach a supermarket.

Here are some of the study's key findings:
- Approximately 24.6 million people, 8% of the total continental U.S. population, live in LSA areas.
- A total of 1,519 LSA areas exist in the continental United States, amounting to 18,639 of the 207,608 block groups (8.98% of block groups) nationwide. These areas are distributed among highly urban communities, small towns and rural areas.
- LSA areas range in size and population density, with the average LSA area measuring 6.4 square miles and having a population of 9,000.
- In the continental United States, a person is 2.49 times more likely to live in an LSA area if that person is Black, non-Hispanic than if that person is White, non-Hispanic.
- A person who is Hispanic is 1.38 times more likely to live in an LSA area than a person who is White, non-Hispanic.
- If one lives in a low-income block group, one is 1.38 times more likely to live in an LSA area than a person living in a non-low-income block group. Low-income block groups are defined as those in which the median household income is less than 80% of area median income or of the relevant non-metro median income.

There are many ways to determine where the problem of store access is most pronounced. For instance, a group wishing to focus on access for minority communities or areas with a high percentage of female-headed households can make use of PolicyMap to identify LSA areas that also meet their other criteria. In this paper, TRF ranks areas based on a composite of two factors, the percentage of total population living in LSA areas and the percentage of total population living in low-income block groups. These factors are consistent with the CDFI Fund's mission to expand access to capital for underserved communities. Based on these two key measures, these areas rank highest:
- On the state level: Pennsylvania, Rhode Island, Louisiana, Connecticut and Illinois

- For cities with populations of over 500,000: Washington, DC; Baltimore, MD; Philadelphia, PA; Dallas, TX and Milwaukee, WI
- For cities of 250,000 to 500,000 people: Cleveland, OH; Kansas City, MO; St. Louis, MO; Newark NJ and Buffalo, NY
- For cities of 100,000 to 250,000 people: Richmond, VA; Knoxville, TN; Syracuse, NY; Baton Rouge, LA and New Haven, CT
- For cities of 50,000 to 100,000 people: Camden, NJ; Trenton, NJ; Gary, IN; Lawrence, MA and Youngstown, OH

This study also measures leakage, which is a measure of unmet local demand for food in LSA areas, an important factor from a retail-industry perspective. The estimated level of leakage provides a way to distinguish between LSA areas that could support a new full-service supermarket or the expansion of an existing store and those areas in which providing other forms of food retail may be a more viable strategy.

Here are some key findings:
- On average, residents living in LSA areas spend $1,120 annually on food products outside of their areas.
- Our analysis of industry data shows that the average full-service supermarket produces $12 million annually in sales.
- TRF identified 772 LSA areas that have an estimated leakage of less than or equal to $12 million and 747 LSA areas that have an estimated leakage of greater than $12 million.

Some LSA areas overlap with census tracts targeted with economic development incentives. This overlap may bring additional resources to a proposed store-development site. Eighty percent of LSA areas are within census tracts that were eligible in 2011 for Community Development Block Grants (CDBGs), and 60% were within areas eligible for the New Markets Tax Credit (NMTC). Each overlap offers significant resources to support interventions.

Using Trade Dimensions data, TRF determined that $12 million is the average annual sales volume for full-service supermarkets. This number is a good benchmark for CDFIs to consider when evaluating whether an LSA area has the required unmet demand to sustain a store. For areas that do not meet the $12 million leakage threshold, the LSA-area population may be small (with a limited amount of unmet demand), or the area may contain numerous alternative stores (including conventional pharmacies) that capture the existing demand for food. Places with leakage below $12 million may still provide an investment opportunity for CDFIs and others to finance the expansion of existing stores, allowing stores to offer a greater diversity of types of foods. Low leakage areas may also represent places where communities can consider programs that increase access through alternative means, such as farmers markets, transportation programs to stores or efforts to support existing stores in expanding their selection of food items.

This document summarizes results related to states and cities based on the income, age and race of those living in LSA areas. These are just a few of the ways in which users of PolicyMap can organize study results to prioritize or characterize LSA areas. The characteristics chosen for the current analysis may not reflect the priorities driven by local needs and resources. Thus PolicyMap allows CDFIs and other users to assemble LSA results with any variables in the database to suit local planning and program-design purposes.

The methodology used in this study to determine LSA areas can be summarized in six steps:

(1)   All block groups in the continental United States were categorized using census data for population density and car ownership. This process resulted in eight density categories, ranging from Density 1 (lowest density—highest car ownership) to Density 8 (highest density—lowest car ownership). Some density categories were further subcategorized based on car-ownership rates.

(2)   Census block groups were used as the geographic unit of analysis. TRF calculated the distance traveled from the population center of every census block to the nearest full-service store.

(3)   Benchmark distances were calculated. The benchmark distance represents a "comparatively acceptable" distance for households to travel to a supermarket. TRF defines a "comparatively acceptable" distance as the distance that residents of well-served areas (with incomes greater than 120% of the area's median income) travel to the nearest supermarket, compared to other residents within the same density category.

Each density category forms a reference group with its own benchmark distance.

(4)   Each block group was assigned an access score. This score represents the percentage that an LSA block group's distance from a supermarket would have to be lowered in order to equal the reference group's distance. Thus a high access score indicates a more pronounced problem.

(5)   Clusters of block groups with high access scores were identified as LSA areas.

(6)   Retail grocery leakage was quantified as a way to determine the magnitude of each LSA area's problem and to estimate unmet demand for food. Leakage was calculated by taking a block group's total demand for food and subtracting sales at existing stores that service the block group. Dollar estimates were then converted to square feet using nationwide weighted averages for sales per square foot among full-service grocers.

Section I: Introduction

Most residents of the United States enjoy a variety of options for purchasing food to eat at home. Yet in some areas, residents have limited access to fresh, healthy foods at a reasonable cost. This limitation can affect both their well-being and their budgets. The U.S. Department of Agriculture's Economic Research Service reports that people without access to full-service grocery stores tend to depend on small grocery or convenience stores that may not carry the variety of foods needed for a healthy diet. It also reports that convenience stores often charge more than grocery stores for the same items, which can deter people from eating a balanced diet.[1]

Clearly, identifying areas in which residents have inadequate food access has the potential to improve public health and quality of life. For these and other reasons, issues of food access have drawn the attention of national and regional policymakers, academia and the media. Beginning in the early 1990s, ample literature has documented areas with inadequate access to retail grocers (areas sometimes referred to as "food deserts"). Yet wide variations in methodology still exist. As a result, those concerned with food access have been unable to reach a consensus about what constitutes an area with inadequate access to healthy food. Public-sector entities, such as economic development agencies, health advocates and community development organizations, may view the issue from varying perspectives, while store operators almost exclusively seek locations that can be profitable. As a community lender, TRF seeks to bridge these gaps by identifying optimal areas for locating stores that meet public-benefit criteria—by increasing adequate access to healthy food—as well as market-viability criteria—by supporting supermarket development where there is sufficient demand to sustain a new store or expand an existing store.

In addition to satisfying local demand for food, supermarkets can bring many economic benefits to communities. They can serve as anchors for additional retail and service-sector businesses, resulting in a viable cluster of employment and commerce, and stores built on previously underused land may increase property and business tax revenues for municipalities. These benefits can be particularly important for areas with inadequate access to healthy food, because these places often face other economic challenges, which can include high vacancy rates, elevated levels of crime, concentrations of households in poverty and limited employment opportunities.

While stores can stimulate economies, we have found that the cost of operating a store in distressed urban markets can limit the development of a new supermarket. TRF's experiences in this area are documented in "Healthy Food Retail Financing at Work,"[2] a chapter in the implementation handbook prepared for the CDFI Fund. Specific market obstacles affect supermarket costs, and these obstacles include both *development costs* (such as land assembly, urban tax policies and higher construction costs) and *location-dependent operating costs* (such as increased requirements for workforce training, employee turnover, security and insurance).[3]

The barriers to entry observed in Philadelphia are consistent with the nationwide reports from operators that are noted in the 2011 "Access to Healthier Foods: Opportunities and Challenges for Food Retailers in Underserved Areas," a report by the Food Marketing Institute (FMI).[4] This report acknowledges that some people lack access to full-service supermarkets and explains that an inadequate demographic base can be an additional challenge for those seeking to attract a supermarket to distressed neighborhoods. The FMI report also notes that not only do many distressed areas have fewer shoppers, but these shoppers have less disposable income than those in other areas. Unlike residents in higher-income communities, shoppers in distressed markets are often unable to purchase the high-margin items that are typically the revenue drivers of supermarkets. In addition, per-shopper expenditures in economically distressed areas are typically lower than those in higher-income areas, which further strains sustainable business models. While opportunity may exist in such markets, operators are challenged to find viable locations or to consider alternative ways to make a store profitable.

Some city, state and federal programs, recognizing the economic benefits of supermarkets, have subsidized the cost of commercial development sites to attract stores to underserved and economically distressed communities. The success of these programs has been judged primarily through the numbers of jobs created, businesses attracted and economies stimulated; increased food access has not been a quantified program benefit. To address this, the Pennsylvania Fresh Food Financing Initiative (FFFI) was created in 2004. FFFI aims to help address the specific financing challenges for supermarkets, and it does so with the primary goal of increasing access to healthy foods. The initiative has financed improvements to existing stores as well as financing the construction of new supermarkets and other retail grocery stores in underserved communities across Pennsylvania. As the fund manager, TRF sought to expand entrepreneurs' ability to become supermarket operators and developers by financing credit needs that could not be fulfilled by conventional financial institutions alone. The success of Pennsylvania's FFFI demonstrates that some distressed areas contain enough unmet demand to support new and/or expanded grocery stores. Once the costs imposed by barriers to entry are offset through financing subsidies, properly placed stores can become profitable, offer economic opportunities to communities and provide a wide diversity of foods.

Inspired by these successes, CDFIs in several states, including New York, California and Illinois, are now creating financing programs similar to the FFFI. The CDFI Fund awarded Healthy Food Financing Initiative financial awards to 25 CDFIS in 2011. As more and more programs are being designed to address inadequate access to supermarkets, the lack of consensus over what constitutes an "underserved community" becomes a pressing matter. Identifying where the problem is most pronounced and determining the appropriate intervention is quite a challenge in this environment.

With the support of the CDFI Fund, TRF has stepped into the gap to provide tools and models that can help programs define their terms and determine their most effective interventions. When FFFI was launched, TRF did not have a tool for assessing need and measuring unmet demand. In an effort to expand our work, support the CDFI community and inform local and national program development, TRF has sought to create a valid and reliable measure of access to healthy food and to subsequently help identify underserved communities.

TRF's LSA results are available on PolicyMap, making it accessible to anyone with internet access. This versatile tool identifies LSA areas nationwide and the magnitude of its access problem and can also highlight each LSA area's demographic characteristics.

In this paper we document our research, methods and results. Prior to performing our study of LSA areas, we reviewed and critiqued existing studies locating "food deserts" and devised ways to resolve these limitations in our study methodology. This paper also offers a description of the methodology used in creating our analysis and a summary of results for states and cities of various sizes (aggregated from census block groups for the continental United States). The conclusion to this document offers a "framework for evaluation" (see page 53) to guide local efforts to evaluate LSA areas and the need for intervention.

This analysis is a practical tool, and all of our results are available at www.policymap.com for all block groups, cities and states within our study area. Taken together, this report and PolicyMap give concerned parties access to valuable data and analytic tools to guide their analysis and decision-making.

Section II: Literature Review

"Food desert" has become a catch-all term in the arena of healthy food-access policy. Most broadly, it describes areas with limited access to certain types of foods or to certain store types. Section 7527 of the 2008 Farm Bill defines a food desert as "an area in the United States with limited access to affordable and nutritious food, particularly such an area composed of predominantly lower-income neighborhoods and communities." [5]

This definition includes four components: a geographical location, a notion of limited access, the concept of sources of affordable and nutritious foods and socioeconomic characteristics. Researchers using the term "food desert" may not consider all of these components in seeking to identify the locations of food deserts, and even when they do, they have used different indicators to measure each component of the definition. The potential food sources considered, for instance, are not standardized; neither is the use of socioeconomic indicators. In addition, access can be defined in absolute terms or in comparison to the access of others.

A 2010 systematic review by Walker, Keane and Burke of the research literature on food deserts finds that the phrase has been inconsistently used, resulting in varied definitions of food deserts and varied assessments of the measures needed to identify them.[6] Despite these differences, however, the reviewers conclude that studies of food access claim strong evidence of significant disparities in access throughout the United States.

The reviewers also found that methodological variations occur at almost every step of the analytic process used to identify food deserts. For instance, studies may differ not only in the types of retail food options they consider, but also in the data sources they use to identify the locations of retail food options. Once an area's food sources and locations are determined, studies then use varying methods to establish whether an area's food offerings are sufficient.

Despite differences in study methods, researchers have drawn similar conclusions that some areas have limited access to healthy foods. A 2010 meta-analysis published in the *Journal of Preventative Chronic Disease* investigates food access through a systematic review of the subject.[7] The authors review the findings of 49 studies from five countries, noting: "Geographic areas with a high proportion of low-income or African American residents were underserved by food retailers compared with more advantaged areas. Evidence is both abundant and robust enough for us to conclude that Americans living in low-income and minority areas tend to have poor access to healthy food." The authors draw these conclusions despite wide variations in measurement across the 49 studies.

Another systematic review, published in the *American Journal of Preventive Medicine*, comes to a similar conclusion. This review considered 54 journal articles from 1985 to 2008 and found that, "despite some inconsistencies, several U.S. studies have shown that residents of rural, low-income, and minority communities are most often affected by poor access to supermarkets, chain grocery stores and healthful food products." Despite acknowledging wide variations in methods, the authors conclude that the studies they review demonstrate disparities in access that were real and substantial. The authors end by stating, "Additional research is needed to address various limitations of current studies, identify effective policy actions and evaluate intervention strategies designed to promote more equitable access to healthy foods." [8]

Heeding the recommendation offered by these authors, TRF sought to devise a methodology for evaluating communities around the nation relative to their specific need for access to supermarkets. We recognized that the analysis would need to be conducted at a highly localized level and that the results must be accessible to the public. While localized, our analysis, must also be systematic to allow results to be aggregated to various levels of geography based upon user preferences. Additionally, the study needed to use consistent, reliable measurements that accommodate for the diversity of communities throughout the country. This next section notes measurements used in prior studies and the limitations associated with these datasets, as well as other factors considered in establishing our methodology.

Using supermarkets as a proxy for access to affordable, healthy foods

Much of the research on food access uses the accessibility of large food retail outlets (e.g., "supermarkets," "chain stores," "midsized or large stores") as a proxy for the availability of affordable, nutritious food. There are widespread assumptions that larger stores such as supermarkets sell affordable, healthy food, and the research on the differences between product options by store type supports these assumptions. A 2009 *Journal of Urban Health* study measures shelf space devoted to fruits and vegetables across different store types in New Orleans and Los Angeles.[9] In addition to comparing absolute shelf space, the authors compare shelf space used for fruits and vegetables to both total store area and space used for unhealthy items. Through both of these relative measurements, the authors find that supermarkets and medium-sized food stores sell significantly greater proportions of healthy foods than small grocery and convenience stores, with supermarkets reporting the highest ratios of healthy to unhealthy foods. The study concludes that "there were large variations between different store types and much smaller variations within individual store types in the absolute and relative shelf length of healthy and unhealthy food items" and that "measurements indicate that store type is a reasonable proxy measure for store contents."

A 2008 *American Journal of Preventive Medicine* study of food availability in the Baltimore area finds similar correlations between store type and availability of nutritious foods.[10] The researchers compute a Healthy Food Availability Index (HFAI), ranking each store's healthy food offerings on a scale of zero to 27 (with 27 being the highest score).[11] Then they compute averages for each store type, as categorized in the InfoUSA directory: supermarkets, grocery stores and convenience stores. Results show that most of the differences in healthy food availability were accounted for between—not within— store types. For instance, their average HFAI score for supermarkets ranges from 18.67 to 24.0, while grocery stores scored from 3.85 to 6.17 and convenience stores ranged from 3.78 to 5.25. While HFAI scores did vary slightly within store types, they varied far more widely among store types, making store type a crucial access factor. The study also showed that the availability of certain types of stores, particularly supermarkets, varies according to a neighborhood's socioeconomic and racial characteristics.

Several other studies corroborate this link between the availability of nutritious food and store type, with supermarkets tending to have the best selection and the highest percentage of affordable, healthy food.[12] Small stores can also be an adequate source of healthy food, particularly in relatively prosperous areas,[13] in immigrant communities,[14] or in stores that have received targeted assistance to provide a wider selection of healthy food items.[15] However, supermarkets have been shown consistently to provide the widest variety of healthy foods and therefore are a reliable proxy for the availability of nutritious foods. As a result, TRF measures access to supermarkets as the proxy for access to healthy foods.

Creating a reliable data source for store locations

Creating an accurate and comprehensive list of supermarkets is an essential first step in supermarket-access research. A store left off the list will result in some areas being inaccurately designated as having inadequate access. Conversely, a store that has closed but that is left on the list will keep areas with inadequate access from being designated as such.

Past researchers have used a variety of resources to locate supermarkets. Data sources fall into roughly three categories: proprietary, public and direct observation. Proprietary sources include databases from Dun & Bradstreet, ReferenceUSA, InfoUSA and Nielsen Trade Dimensions, which offer nationwide data on supermarket locations. Such proprietary data generally must be purchased, and sources vary in quality and accuracy. Public data sources include Yellow Pages, other telephone directories and city or state databases. Studies comparing store-location data from Dun and Bradstreet, InfoUSA and state government registries have found discrepancies among the datasets.[16,17] Direct observation is highly useful for localized research but is not feasible for a national research project. Among these sources, then, TRF has found Trade Dimensions to be most accurate and has made use of this data for our LSA study. USDA also selected Trade Dimensions as the source for the supermarket data to complete the study called "Access to Affordable and Nutritious Food: Measuring and Understanding Food Deserts and Their Consequences."[18]

Another limitation to consider is that some datasets do not provide enough information on the types and sizes of stores for users to determine access to full-service supermarkets exclusively. Most data sources rely on SIC or NAICS codes to provide store classifications and use self-reported or estimated sales figures. An NAICS code of 445110 refers to "Supermarkets and Other Grocery (except Convenience) Stores" and "comprises establishments generally known as supermarkets and grocery stores primarily engaged in retailing a general line of food, such as canned and frozen foods; fresh fruits and vegetables; and fresh and prepared meats, fish, and poultry. Included in this industry classification are delicatessen-type establishments primarily engaged in retailing a general line of food."[19] This shows clearly that datasets providing only NAICS codes will not enable users to isolate full-service grocery stores.

Using distance as a measure of access

After identifying supermarket locations in a given area, a researcher must determine the degree of supermarket access experienced by residents. An operational definition of low access is essential for distinguishing legitimately underserved areas. In most studies, distance to a supermarket is used as a proxy for food accessibility and is measured directly from point to point in a straight-line fashion; some studies have measured distance along street grids to obtain the real-life travel or "network" distance.[20]

In using distance to estimate food access, researchers have typically used one distance or several fixed distances to measure access of residents within a designated study area to the nearest grocer. Other measures consider a store accessible to a block group if a store is located within that block group's boundaries.[21] Researchers also try to determine variety by noting the presence of multiple accessible food retailers in an area, either through a simple count of retailers within a fixed radius[22] or by creating a "heat map" that reflects both distance to food retail and the presence of multiple food retail outlets.[23]

The use of distance as a proxy for food access, although intuitive, presents a significant problem because no one distance to a supermarket is appropriate for all neighborhoods. Neighborhoods vary widely in terms of both their built environments and their residents' access to transportation. A reasonable distance to food for residents in one neighborhood might be a prohibitive distance for residents in another. Some past research recognizes this and proposes different distance buffers for walking and driving, taking account of transit access[24] or neighborhood walkability[25] in order to correlate those development patterns with observed distance to food sources. However, no known prior research has systematically varied—on a national scale—the factor of travel distances to account for both a wide diversity in neighborhood population-density categories and a range in residents' access to cars. The Economic Research Service (ERS/USDA) Food Desert Locator[26] provides two distances, one for urban and one for rural areas, but it does not account for the considerable diversity among urban and rural areas or neighborhoods.

Knowing the difference between absolute and relative measures of access

Prior studies have used either relative or absolute measures of access. A relative measure is one that compares the level of access in each geographic area to the level of access for one subgroup of the total study population. This subgroup constitutes a reference group. For example, in "Food Store Availability and Neighborhood Characteristics," Powell, Slater et al. compare the level of access in low-income zip codes to that of high-income zip codes.[27] Low access in this particular study is therefore relative to the access of an area's high-income group.

Absolute measures of access are based on a fixed distance threshold only. The recent USDA study published by the Economic Research Service (ERS/USDA) as a part of a 2009 report to Congress[28] uses an absolute measure of access, measuring distance from population to the nearest source of healthy foods[29] by dividing the land area for the nation into 1-kilometer-square grids and assessing each cell area's level of access. A later release of the data on the USDA's Food Desert Locator website identifies census tracts as low access if at least 33% of its residents (or 500 residents, whichever is larger) live more than 1 mile from a supermarket or large grocery store in urban areas or 10 miles in rural areas. Another national study, conducted by Environmental Systems Research Institute, Inc., uses an absolute distance, defining limited access as census blocks with distance to a store of greater than a 10-minute walk or drive.[30]

The choice between relative verses absolute is important because each provides vastly different low-access-population estimates. After an appropriate reference distance (absolute or relative) is determined, researchers consider the issues of the measurement scale. The low-access scale could be nominal (categorical), ordinal or both. A nominal low-access scale is one for which an area is defined as low access with "Yes" or "No." An ordinal score evaluation is one for which the degree of the access problem is measured by how different access is for the low-access area from that of the non-low-access area.

Measuring demand for food

Relatively little research has gone from designating an area as low access to describing the market opportunities within these areas based on a determination of leakage. Other than TRF's prior study of supermarket access, we are unaware of any studies that have assessed both low access and leakage for the continental United States. Understanding the economic landscape within a given low-access area is important because this knowledge can help parties identify viable strategies for increasing access to healthy food for its residents. From the retail-industry perspective, unmet or inadequately met local demand can be a strong indicator of market opportunity.

Leakage is defined in financial terms as "a measure of retail sales lost by a community to a competitive market, indicating the need for more retail development in an area." [31] Sales leaked out of an area are presumed to result in the loss of economic activity, jobs and perhaps tax revenue (if sales are made in a neighboring jurisdiction), and thus lost sales represent the unmet demand within a community. Different methods are used to estimate both general retail leakage and leakage broken down by sectors (such as grocery leakage). [32] The Social Compact's Grocery Gap Analysis quantified low-access areas using U.S. census "market basket" expenditures, a measure that covers a broad range of items beyond food. [33]

The most widely accepted method for calculating grocery leakage compares sales receipts within a given area with estimated spending in that area. Actual sales figures are sometimes collected from the U.S. Economic Census. [34] Estimates of potential spending are typically based on data from the U.S. Bureau of Labor Statistics' Consumer Expenditure Survey, which collects information on the purchasing habits of households in different income categories and regions. These estimates are then multiplied by household counts to calculate demand within an area. Leakage compares available sales figures with potential sales that an area could support. If actual sales within a market area are lower than projected sales, spending is presumably leaking out of the area, taking away jobs, economic activity and, in the case of adjacent municipal boundaries, perhaps tax revenue. [35] Since leakage measurements assign a dollar amount to unmet demand, they can suggest the scale of new retail needed to satisfy local demand.

While it is important to improve access, not all areas with inadequate access have the market potential to support a new full-service supermarket. Further, the opening of a new store is likely to affect the revenue of existing stores within a city or region. The supermarket industry is highly competitive, with relatively low profit margins compared to other industries. [36] According to the Food Marketing Institute, "the typical grocery store's profit after taxes is approximately 1.3%, with the average store taking in approximately $6,000 per week in profits based upon median [weekly] sales of $466,000." [37] The estimated level of leakage provides interested parties with a way to distinguish between low-access areas that could support a new full-service supermarket and those in which providing other forms of food retail might be a more viable, sustainable strategy. For areas that can support a new full-service supermarket, the potential economic benefits that grocery stores can bring to their communities serve as a strong incentive for intervention.

Section III: Methodology for Identifying Limited Supermarket Access (LSA) Areas

As discussed in the literature review, researchers have defined differing measurements for each component of an LSA analysis. Our study of LSA areas is designed specifically to address this situation by doing the following:

(1)   Establishing a valid and reliable method for measuring areas with inadequate access within the continental United States;

(2)   Locating geographic areas with the strongest need for additional supermarket development and quantifying the demand for the area;

(3)   Allowing for LSA areas to be prioritized based on the degree to which they lack access, have grocery demand and experience retail leakage; and

(4)   Offering a mapping tool to allow a diverse range of clients, including government agencies, lending institutions, communities and policy research organizations, to analyze LSA areas within their geographies and to craft strategies based on conditions in their communities.

Definition of areas with low access to healthy, affordable food

This study defines places with inadequate supermarket access as areas in which residents must travel significantly farther to the nearest full-service grocery store than residents of areas showing similar population density and car-ownership characteristics as well as median household incomes greater than 120% of the area median. What follows is an explanation of how this definition was executed into a quantitative low-access measure for the continental United States. The sources of data used to perform the analysis are also provided.

Unit of analysis: TRF's methodology uses census block groups as the unit of analysis. The analysis included two key components for estimating the true distance that residents travel. First, 2010 U.S. Census block centroids (population center of a block group) were used as the starting location of the distance calculation. Census blocks are the smallest geography at which the U.S. Census Bureau provides population counts and thus provides a more accurate spatial depiction of population locations. Block groups also offer detailed information about the built environment and car-ownership rates while still representing a spatially concentrated population, making them the appropriate geography at which to consider food-access interventions. Census block groups also provide a relatively consistent measure of population for which associated socioeconomic, demographic and car-ownership data are available. While TRF does not factor demographic or ethnicity data into the analysis, using block groups also allows this descriptive information to be available after designation for assessing appropriate programmatic intervention.

The 2010 Census includes 6,182,882 blocks with a population greater than zero. TRF spatially matched the 2000 Census block group boundaries and the 2010 block centroids to aggregate individual blocks' travel distance to the 2000 block group boundaries. This was necessary because the ancillary datasets (data providing car ownership and mean household income) are currently only available for the 2000 Census block groups. Our study area was limited to the 2000 Census block groups for the continental United States (207,608 block groups), which have an average population of 1,481 people with a standard deviation[38] of 1,377.

TRF utilizes car-ownership data (2000 Census)[39] and income data (2005-2009 American Community Survey) as components for establishing access. Since datasets from the census are collected through surveys and represent a population sample from each block group, results at the block group level are generally subject to greater sampling variations than at higher levels of geography. This is especially true for block groups with very small populations. Without a standard to guide the exclusion of block groups based on population, we chose to eliminate block groups with populations less than or equal to 250 or less than 100 households, a total of 1.8% of all census block groups, equaling 3,838 people.

Location of supermarkets: Trade Dimensions is a proprietary nationwide database of individual food and drug store listings used for this analysis. The data represents stores in operation as of March 1, 2011 and includes 50,602 grocery stores.[40] Of these, 37,240 (73.6%) are considered full-service supermarkets and were included in the analysis. The information in the database, including store location, latitude and longitude, annual sales and square footage information, was used to spatially locate supermarkets nationwide and as a part of our supply calculation of retail grocery leakage.

Our objective is to use data as the industry itself does to characterize market potential, so that the results can then be used by practitioners to evaluate opportunities. The USDA's Congressionally commissioned report, the only other known national study, also used the Trade Dimensions database to locate supermarkets.[41] Unlike other commercial datasets, Trade Dimensions is a nationwide industry database that specifically categorizes food retail outlets (supermarkets, small grocery stores known as superettes, convenience stores, wholesale clubs, etc.) and gathers data from a variety of sources; other data sources rely on self-reporting mechanisms. Use of Trade Dimensions data has the additional benefit of using store-type classifications that are consistent with the Food Marketing Institute's (FMI) classifications.[42] Trade Dimensions utilizes the trade channel definition endorsed by FMI and leading industry publications. A full description of all store types and the Trade Dimensions definitions are included in Appendix 1. Table 1 displays the number of stores by the categories used in this analysis and defines store characteristics by type.

For this study, the full-service supermarket classification serves as the proxy for availability of affordable and nutritious food. The list of full-service supermarkets includes conventional supermarkets, limited assortment stores, supercenters, natural/gourmet foods, warehouse stores, military commissary stores[43] and conventional/ wholesale clubs. Based on the literature review referenced earlier, our analysis excludes superette/ small grocery stores because typically they either do not provide a full line of perishable foods or they do so at prices that are higher than those at larger stores.[44,45,46]

In TRF's previous analysis in 2010, we excluded limited assortment stores from our full-service list due to our assessment that these stores did not provide the range of fresh produce, dairy and meat products available at supermarkets. Since our original analysis, however, data released on current market trends from FMI suggests that, due to the national economic downturn, limited assortment stores (traditionally seen as "bargain shopper" stores) have become more attractive to a larger segment of the population and now provide a selection of fresh foods. Limited assortment market-share expansion is reflected in annual customers' surveys administered by FMI. When asked for their "primary store choice or the store where shoppers spend the majority of their grocery budget," the percentage of responses citing limited assortment stores has risen from 1% in 2005 to 3% in 2009 and 7% in 2010.[47] Additionally, data in Table 1 demonstrates that limited assortment stores represent 3% of the total full-service grocery-store sales and 5% of the average store type grocery sales.[48] With this market-share expansion, these types of stores have also expanded their product lines to include additional fresh produce, dairy and meat options. A review of limited assortment store websites, recent news articles and circulars demonstrates that their product selection is now more similar to that of small full-service supermarkets.[49] For these reasons, TRF included limited assortment stores in this analysis.

Table 1:
2011 Retail Grocery Characteristics by Store Category (as defined by Trade Dimensions)

Description	Number of Stores	Total Food Sales ($1,000)	Total Square Feet for Food Sales	Average Grocery Sales	Average Grocery Sq Ft	Sales Per Square Foot
Conventional Club	1,201	39,879,320	46,348,000	33,205,096	38,591	860
Conventional Drug	20,549	14,405,872	33,785,000	701,050	1,644	426
Military Commissary	175	3,567,408	4,463,000	20,385,189	25,503	799
Supercenter	3,478	80,806,336	86,582,000	23,233,564	24,894	933
Superette	13,009	15,654,548	34,749,000	1,203,363	2,671	451
Supermarket, Conventional	26,641	318,296,732	640,530,000	11,947,627	24,043	497
Supermarket, Limited Assortment	2,841	12,837,240	33,050,000	4,518,564	11,633	388
Supermarket, Natural/Gourmet Foods	2,422	20,258,992	19,859,000	8,364,571	8,199	1,020
Warehouse Grocery	482	3,445,104	8,330,000	7,147,519	17,282	414
Total	*70,798*	*509,151,552*	*907,696,000*	*7,191,609*	*12,821*	*561*
Total less Conventional Drug	*50,249*	*494,745,680*	*873,911,000*	*9,845,881*	*17,392*	*566*
*Full-Service Stores Only**	*37,240*	*479,091,132*	*839,162,000*	*12,864,961*	*22,534*	*571*

Represents stores included in the analysis Store types are in bold are included n the full-service category.

Steps of the LSA Analysis

While there are many interim steps in TRF's process of analysis, the overall process can be defined by six methodological steps. Anyone interested in viewing each step that went into the analysis can do so via www.trfund.com or at www.policymap.com.

Step I: Classify Population Density/Car-Ownership Rate Categorize all block groups in the continental United States into subgroups using census data for population density and car ownership. Categorization results in 13 classifications with eight density categories, ranging from Density 1 (lowest density/high car ownership) to Density 8 (highest density/lowest car ownership). Some groups were then further subcategorized based on car-ownership rates. As discussed earlier, prior research has assumed that using one distance as the desirable distance to a grocery store is appropriate for all neighborhoods. From a review of census population-density data, we concluded that a single designation or even a dual (rural and urban) designation does not represent the variety within the continental United States. Access to supermarkets varies based on how densely populated an area is and on the rate of car ownership (along with factors beyond the scope of this analysis). Further, the selected distance benchmarks used to represent optimal distances should represent places in which the market operates optimally.

TRF's methodology systematically varies the appropriate travel distances for census block groups based on population density and, in denser areas on car-ownership rates. Controlling for population density is important because, with all else being equal, increased population density tends to increase total consumer demand in an area and makes an area able to support a higher concentration of commercial ventures. In high-density areas, therefore, one would expect travel distances to supermarkets to be shorter than in low-density areas. Car-ownership rates are also an important factor because vehicle ownership changes travel time drastically (and travel time is the true indicator of access, for which distance attempts to account). Thus car ownership can significantly influence food-shopping habits.[50]

TRF divided census block groups into 13 comparison groups based on various combinations of population density and car-ownership rates. Density is based on population data from the 2010 Census (PL-94) and was used to rank all block groups on a scale of 1 to 8. TRF used 2000 Census data for percentage of car ownership[51] to classify block groups within each density category into a series of subcategories (Low Car, Medium Car, High Car, and Very High Car).[52]

Table 2, displays the results of this categorization. Table 2 also highlights the block group characteristics of each density/car-ownership category. Categories 1, 2, 3 and 4 are defined solely by density and were not further split by car ownership. In these very low-density block groups (rural areas), average car-ownership rates exceed 90%. While we recognize the existence of rural block groups with low car-ownership rates, there are so few of these areas that it was statistically inappropriate to split them into a subcategory. As a result, we chose to define the most rural areas by density alone.

More than 50% of the U.S. population falls into density category 7. This category is divided into subgroups to distinguish between the wide variations in car access within U.S. cities and communities. Density/car classification 7VHC represents areas in which 99% of the residents within the block groups have a car and 1.3% have no access to a car. This is in stark contrast to 7LC, in which only 55% of households have access to a car and 45% do not.

Table 2:
Characteristics of Each Category of Population Density and Car Ownership

Population Density/Car Classification	# of Block Groups	% of Block Groups	Total US Population	% of US Total Population	Average % w/o Car
1 Lowest Density, High Car	732	0.4%	539,883	0.2%	4.3%
2 High Car	3,844	1.9%	3,466,507	1.1%	4.8%
3 High Car	10,736	5.3%	12,140,678	4.0%	5.6%
4 High Car	13,991	6.9%	19,529,343	6.4%	5.4%
5 High Car	24,122	11.8%	43,181,357	14.2%	3.8%
5 Medium Car	4,215	2.1%	5,281,715	1.7%	16.2%
6 High Car	26,594	13.1%	54,108,808	17.7%	2.6%
6 Medium Car	14,834	7.3%	18,996,117	6.2%	14.8%
7 Very High Car	22,536	11.1%	37,327,413	12.2%	1.3%
7 High Car	37,502	18.4%	54,544,317	17.9%	6.7%
7 Medium Car	28,983	14.2%	36,880,477	12.1%	18.2%
7 Low Car	13,373	6.6%	14,591,007	4.8%	45.0%
8 Highest Density	2,308	1.1%	4,486,338	1.5%	68.9%
All	203,770	100%	305,073,959	100.0%	10.7%

Note: Only block groups with Census 2010 (PL94) population greater than 250 and household count greater than 100 were classified.

Example: Philadelphia, PA

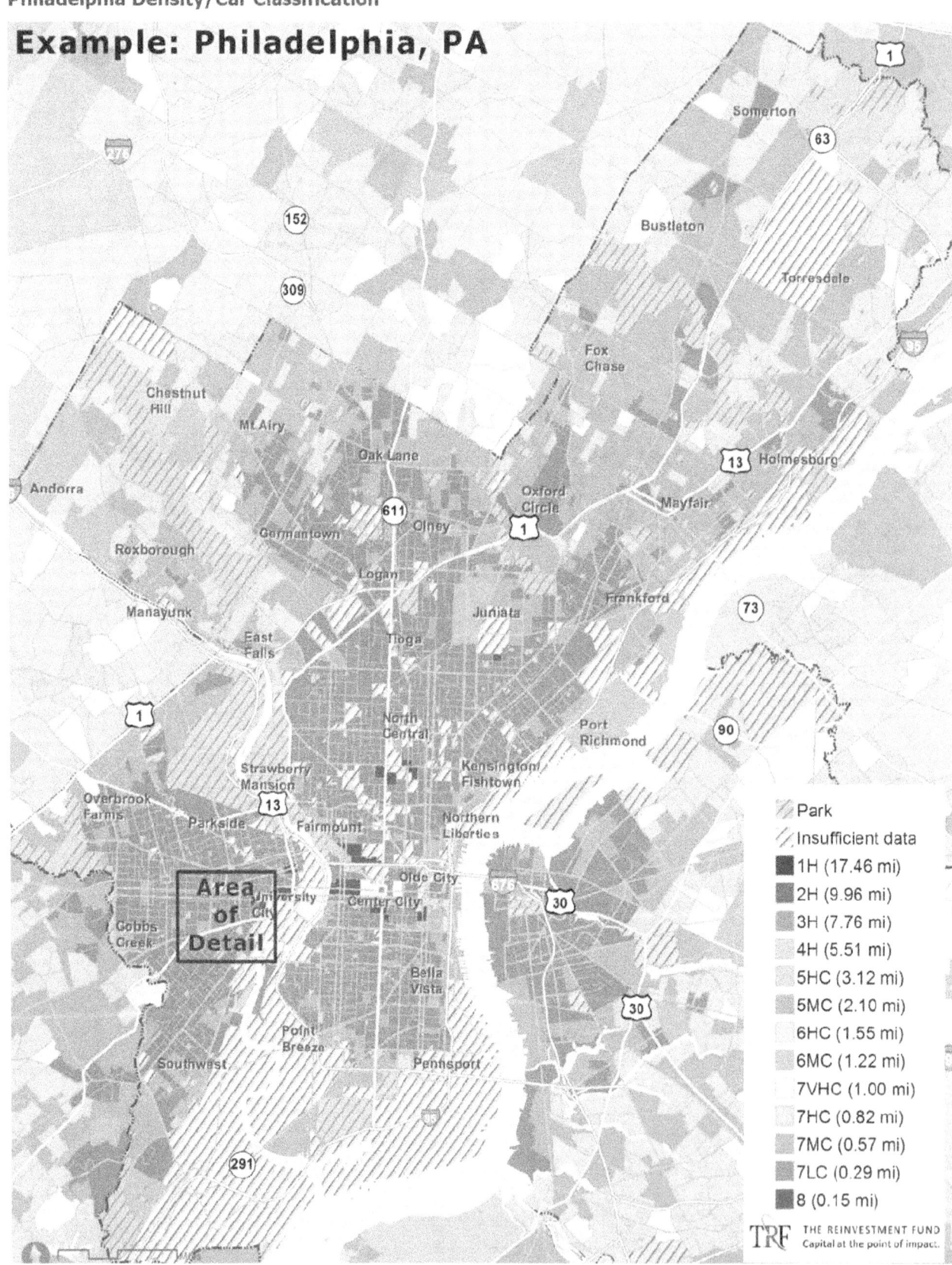

Legend:

- Park
- Insufficient data
- 1H (17.46 mi)
- 2H (9.96 mi)
- 3H (7.76 mi)
- 4H (5.51 mi)
- 5HC (3.12 mi)
- 5MC (2.10 mi)
- 6HC (1.55 mi)
- 6MC (1.22 mi)
- 7VHC (1.00 mi)
- 7HC (0.82 mi)
- 7MC (0.57 mi)
- 7LC (0.29 mi)
- 8 (0.15 mi)

TRF THE REINVESTMENT FUND
Capital at the point of impact.

Map 1 shows the 13 Density/Car categories for Philadelphia and the surrounding area. The area contains categories from 5MC to 8.

It is important to remember that this classification applies to urban, rural and suburban communities. For example, within the boundaries of Philadelphia, PA 9 of the 13 population classifications exist, including from 5MC to 8HC.

Map 2 shows the results for the census block groups in the area of detail. While the majority of census block groups are 7LC, the area also contains some block groups that are 7HC and 8.

Map 2:
Area of Detail

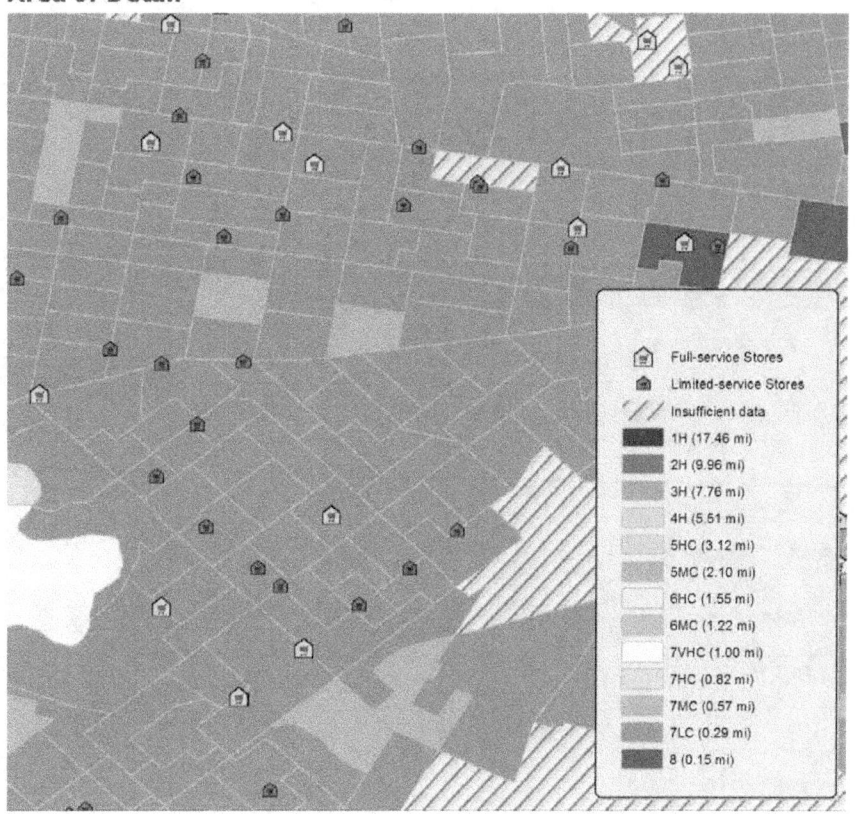

Step II: Calculate Distance to Stores

Calculate the travel distance from the population center of every census block (or block centroid) to the nearest full-service store. Then, for each census block group, establish a population-weighted distance using actual road-travel distance for each of the member blocks.

TRF calculated the distance from the population center of every census block (or block centroid) to the nearest full-service store. The block results were then aggregated to the census block group, establishing a population-weighted distance using actual travel distance on the existing road network for each of the member blocks. This distance value at the block group level is used for all subsequent calculations in the analysis. Distance to the nearest store is calculated using network distance rather than straight-line distance. Network distance finds the path along the existing road system leading to the nearest store and calculates the distance traveled.[53] In contrast, straight-line distance does not consider roads and physical barriers to travel; instead, it calculates the shortest distance from a centroid to its nearest store. Since TRF's network distance calculations account for road connectivity and physical barriers to travel, they provide a more realistic estimate of travel distance to a supermarket. Consider, for example, a population located on one side of a mountain and a store on the other side. Straight-line distance calculates an unreasonably short distance that runs straight through the mountain, while network distance follows roads that lead over or around the mountain. Map 3 shows travel distance to the nearest supermarket.

Map 3:
Travel Distance to Nearest Supermarket

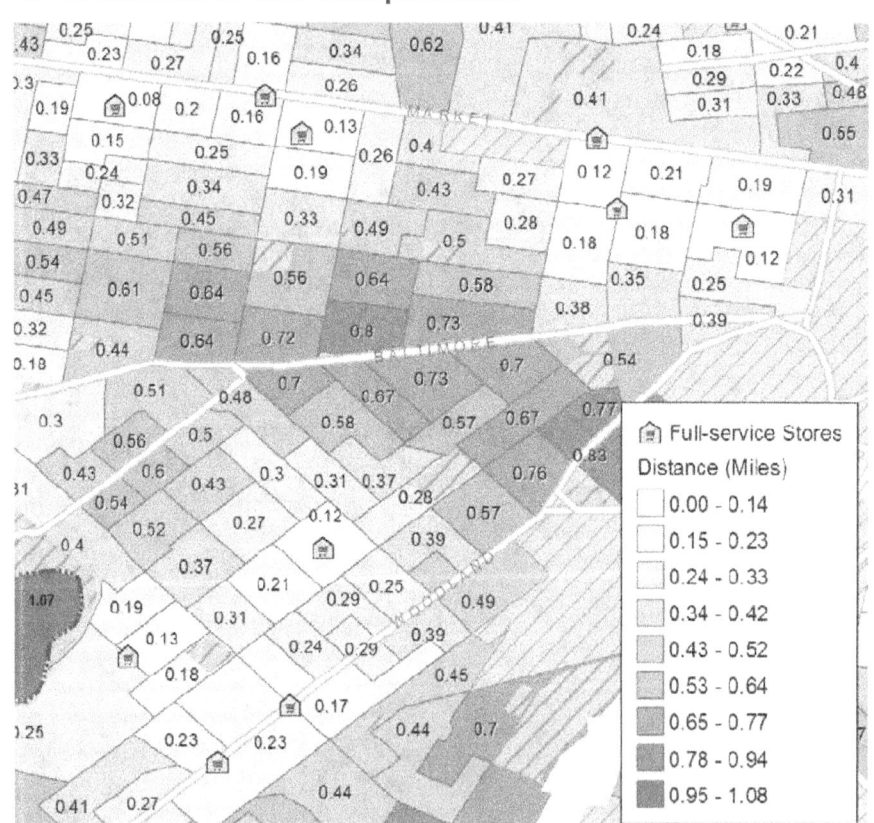

Map 3 displays the actual distance from each block group to the nearest store. The area is densely populated, with the actual distance varying from 0.25 miles to 1.07 miles.

Step III: Establish Benchmark Distances

TRF assumes that block groups with an Area Median Income (AMI) above 120% are adequately served and calculates benchmark reference distances using only these block groups. Each benchmark distance represents the median distance of all block groups to their nearest supermarket within each category created in Step I. The benchmark distance represents a comparatively acceptable distance for households to travel to a supermarket.

An empirically validated, appropriate distance to supermarkets is more sensitive to real-world experiences and market conditions than the arbitrary, fixed-distance benchmarks used in much of the existing research. Therefore, the goal of this step is to define areas with adequate access based on the actual distance travelled to stores and to apply those distances universally to all block groups across the nation, while still controlling for variations in population density and car ownership. Existing research and market trends portray the supermarket industry as extremely competitive, especially in areas with more disposable income per household. Areas that are not economically distressed present the fewest barriers to market penetration and offer the greatest potential for consumer demand. For this reason, our principal assumption in the LSA methodology is that block groups with median household incomes that are greater than 120% of their respective metro area household medians (or non-metro state medians, for non-metro areas) represent the well-served comparison group.[54]

The average actual distances to the closest store for well-served block groups were calculated, and these averages were then established as benchmarks for each of the 13 block group classifications. Table 3 below shows the benchmark differences for higher-income block groups in each of the density/car-ownership categories. The distances vary from .15 miles for block groups in the highest density category to 17.46 miles for areas in the lowest density category.

Table 3:
Benchmark Distance to Nearest Supermarket

	Category	Benchmark Reference Distance in Miles
	1 Lowest Density, High Car	17.46
	2 High Car	9.96
	3 High Car	7.76
	4 High Car	5.51
	5 High Car	3.12
	5 Medium Car	2.1
	6 High Car	1.55
	6 Medium Car	1.22
	7 Very High Car	1
	7 High Car	0.82
	7 Medium Car	0.57
	7 Low Car	0.29
	8 Highest Density	0.15

Note: The median network distance (miles) to nearest store was calculated from the block centroid for only those block groups above 120% AMI.

Step IV: Assign Access Scores

TRF calculates an access score for each block group, which represents the percentage that a block group's distance to its nearest supermarket needs to be reduced in order to equal the benchmark distance.

The analysis compares each block group's travel distance to the reference distances established in Step III to determine whether or not the area has inadequate access. Block groups receive a positive or a negative access score. The score represents the percentage decrease the block group must travel to make its distance to the nearest supermarket equal to that of its well-served peers (those sharing similar population density and car-ownership rates). Negative scores represent those areas with adequate access; positive scores distinguish areas as having low access and estimate the degree of the problem.

For example, if a block group is assigned the 5M density/car-ownership classification and has a network distance to a full-service grocery of 4.5 miles and the 5M reference distance is 2.1 miles, then the access score will be calculated as (4.5-2.1)/4.5 = 0.53. This block group's travel distance would have to be decreased by 53% to equal the distance traveled by its higher-income counterparts. The block groups' access scores represent a ratio scale for which zero represents a complete absence of an equity issue. A zero score means that the distance is less than or equal to the reference distance. For easier utilization of the data on PolicyMap, all negative scores are converted to zero. Higher scores indicate greater inequity compared to the reference group, normalized to a scale of 1 to 100 for comparative analysis. This measure is calculated for all block groups and creates a quantitative measure of the degree to which a block group is underserved by supermarkets. Map 4 shows how much farther households in a block group must travel to access a full-service store based on the benchmark distance.

**Map 4:
Access Score**

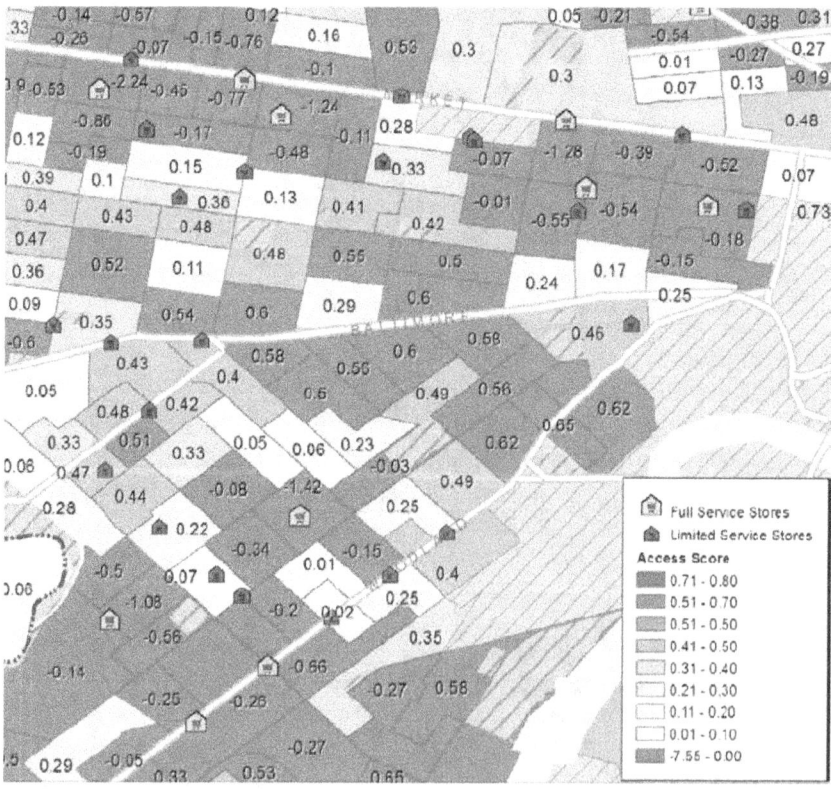

Low access scores displayed on Map 4 show how much farther than their benchmark distance the households must travel to a full-service store. A score converts to percentage of decrease in distance. A high score (highest range is 0.71 - 0.81) represents greater inequity.

Step V: Identify Clusters of LSA areas

TRF uses spatial-statistical methods to identify clusters of block groups with high access scores. These are identified as LSA areas and represent areas with the strongest concentrations of areas with positive access scores.

Block groups are grouped into LSA areas via a spatial-statistical analysis known as Local Indicators of Spatial Association (LISA).[55] This process identifies the presence or absence of significant spatial clusters of block groups with limited access. In essence, LISA takes each block group with a positive access score and compares its score with that of its neighboring block groups (defined as block groups that share a boundary and that also have a road that allows travel between the two) and combines those block groups into an LSA area if their access scores are highly correlated.

This process identifies where the low-access problem is concentrated, which is necessary for the next step of measuring the unmet demand. While a single block group with a high score is a problem for those individuals, it is not likely to warrant a supermarket intervention. In contrast, LSA areas that consist of multiple block groups

may represent a viable market opportunity and require further investigation.

Of all the block groups analyzed, 97,745 (48%) have distances to the nearest supermarket that are equal to or less than their corresponding reference group distances; these block groups are assigned an access score of zero. Table 4, located below, shows block group characteristics by access score range, including figures illustrating each range's share of all block groups (*% of All Block Groups*), all LSA block groups (*% of All LSA Block Groups*), and the percentage of each range's block groups that became part of an LSA area during the spatial clustering process (*LSA Conversion Rate*). A comparison of the *LSA Conversion Rate* among score ranges shows that block groups with scores above 60 are much more likely to become part of an LSA area. For example, only 22% (3,243 of 15,002) of all block groups with an access score between 40.1 and 50 are part of an LSA cluster, compared to 71% (2,748 of 3,865) of block groups with access scores between 70.1 and 80. In other words, block groups with access scores between 70.1 and 80 are over three times more likely to become an LSA-area member than those with scores between 40.1 and 50.

Table 4:
Block Group Counts by Access Score and by LSA Clusters

Access Score	All Block Groups	% of All Block Groups	LSA Block Groups	% of All LSA Block Groups	LSA Conversion Rate
0	97,745	48.0%	0	0.0%	0.0%
0.1 - 10	15,610	7.7%	195	1.0%	1.2%
10.1 - 20	16,934	8.3%	382	2.0%	2.3%
20.1 - 30	17,693	8.7%	679	3.6%	3.8%
30.1 - 40	16,984	8.3%	1,805	9.7%	10.6%
40.0 - 50	15,002	7.4%	3,243	17.4%	21.6%
50.1 - 60	11,176	5.5%	4,284	23.0%	38.3%
60.1 - 70	7,092	3.5%	4,015	21.5%	56.6%
70.1 - 80	3,865	1.9%	2,748	14.7%	71.1%
80.1 - 90	1,478	0.7%	1,129	6.1%	76.4%
90.1 - 100	191	0.1%	159	0.9%	83.2%
Total	203,770	100.0%	18,639	100.0%	9.1%

See Appendix 3 for complete table.

Once LSA areas are identified, TRF calculates population-weighted access scores to account for the variation in populations within block groups. As with the block group access scores, the weighted LSA-area access score provides a quantitative measure of each LSA area's relative disadvantage. These scores represent an ordinal measure, offering a way to rank and prioritize LSA areas based on the severity of the access problem. The population-weighted access scores are available to the public through PolicyMap. (See Map 5.)

Map 5:
Variation in Access Scores Within LSA areas

Map 5 displays the LSA area it is defined by the yellow boundary. The LSA area and its member block groups are the results of the LISA analysis. Low access scores displayed on this map show how much farther than their benchmark distance the households must travel to access a full-service store. A score converts to percentage of decrease distance in. A high score (highest range seen here is 0.71 - 0.80) represents greater inequity.

Step VI: Estimate Grocery Leakage

A leakage figure represents an estimate of the unmet demand for food. It is calculated by assessing both the demand for food (how much residents currently spent on food) and the supply of food (existing food sales). The difference between these figures represents the unmet demand or leakage.

TRF calculated retail grocery leakage for each block group and each LSA area as a means of estimating the magnitude of unmet grocery demand and the corresponding opportunity for additional grocery sales within an area. For block groups with positive access

scores, leakage represents grocery purchases made at full-service stores located beyond a block group's reference distance. It is calculated by subtracting existing food sales from the estimated demand for food.

Estimating demand: The percentage of income that households spend on food prepared at home varies by income level. TRF estimates grocery demand for each block group using household income projections from 2010 Claritas and their corresponding percentage of income spent on "food at home" from the 2009 Bureau of Labor Statistics Consumer Expenditure Survey. (See Map 6.)

Map 6:
Demand for Food

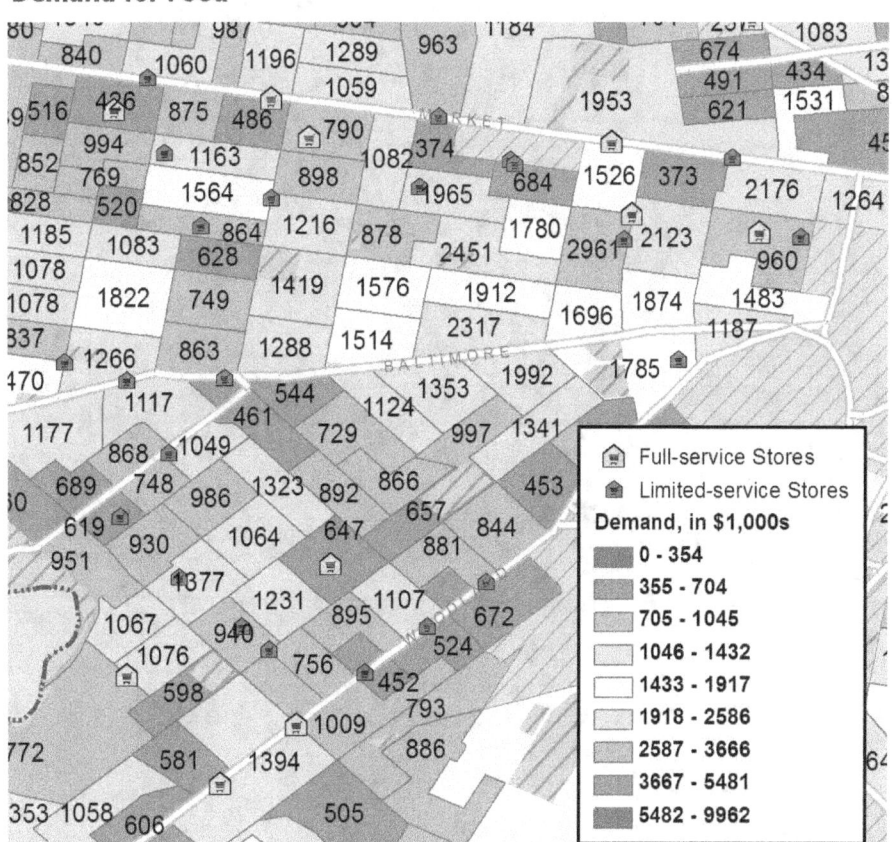

In Map 6, demand represents food expenditures for food prepared at home. This is the first step in the leakage calculation.

Estimating supply: There are currently over 13,000 superettes and 20,549 conventional drug stores operating in TRF's LSA study area; TRF recognizes that these limited-service stores play a role in satisfying grocery demand. The analysis allocates grocery sales from these stores located within a block group's reference distance to the member blocks. Retail grocery sales figures (the grocery "supply" component) are reported for each store in the Trade Dimension database. Each store's food sales are allocated—on a population-weighted basis—to census blocks that contain the store(s) within their reference distance. (See Map 7.)

Map 7:
Food Sales Captured by Area Stores (Supply)

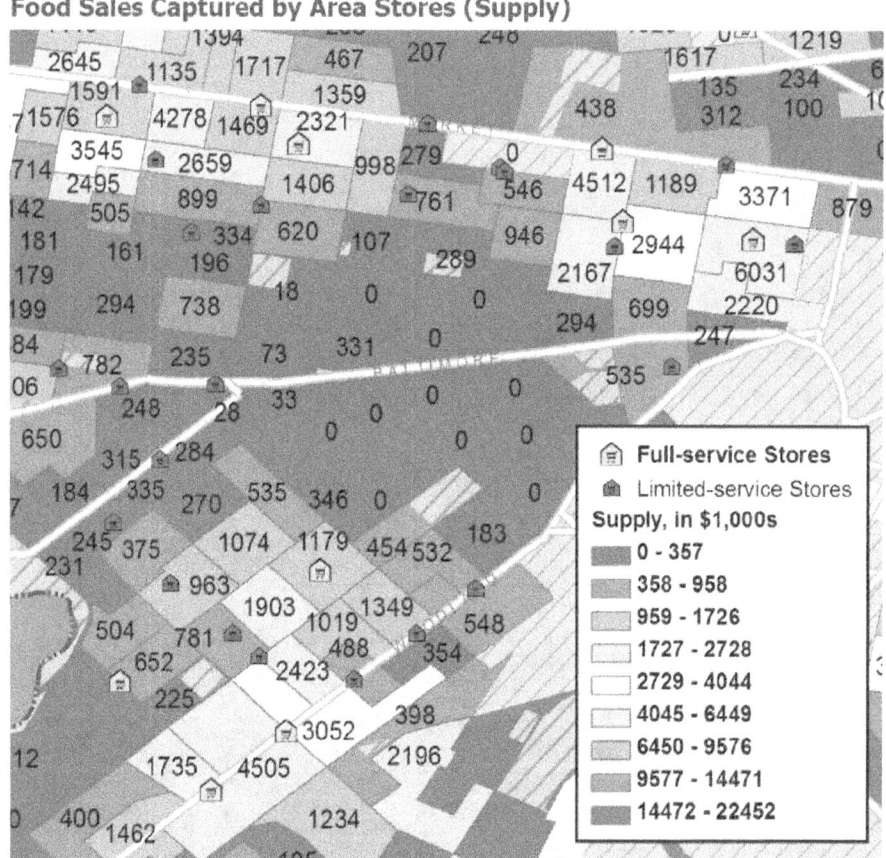

In Map 7, store sales (which reflect supply) are allocated to the member blocks and aggregated to the block group.

Legend:
- Full-service Stores
- Limited-service Stores

Supply, in $1,000s
- 0 - 357
- 358 - 958
- 959 - 1726
- 1727 - 2728
- 2729 - 4044
- 4045 - 6449
- 6450 - 9576
- 9577 - 14471
- 14472 - 22452

Estimating leakage: Lastly, grocery supply is subtracted from demand to estimate retail grocery leakage.[56] Since the access problem is often easier to understand in terms of square footage, TRF converted dollars leaked into square feet of retail space by calculating nationwide averages for grocery sales per square foot among full-service stores (excluding superettes and chain pharmacies). When stated in terms of square feet, the leakage measure helps communities understand the extent of their retail grocery shortage and start to think about the appropriate scale of intervention. Leakage results are used with data regarding supermarket types, size and average annual sales. This format can help those wishing to create strategies for appropriate intervention. (See Map 8.) For a more detailed visual depiction of how sales are allocated in leakage to individual blocks and their block groups, please see Appendix 2.

Map 8:
Demand Minus Supply Equals Leakage

The leakage map shows, in thousands of dollars, the estimated unmet demand for food prepared at home. The areas in blue highlight the places with the highest demand for a new store. Current store locations are on the map as well. The core LSA shows a leakage sum of $27,691,000 (defined in blue). Depending on the placement of the store and its attractiveness to consumers, the demand may capture additional revenue from the unmet demand in the adjacent block groups. These are noted in yellow. Negative leakage indicates that more sales are occurring in that block group than the estimated demand for food.

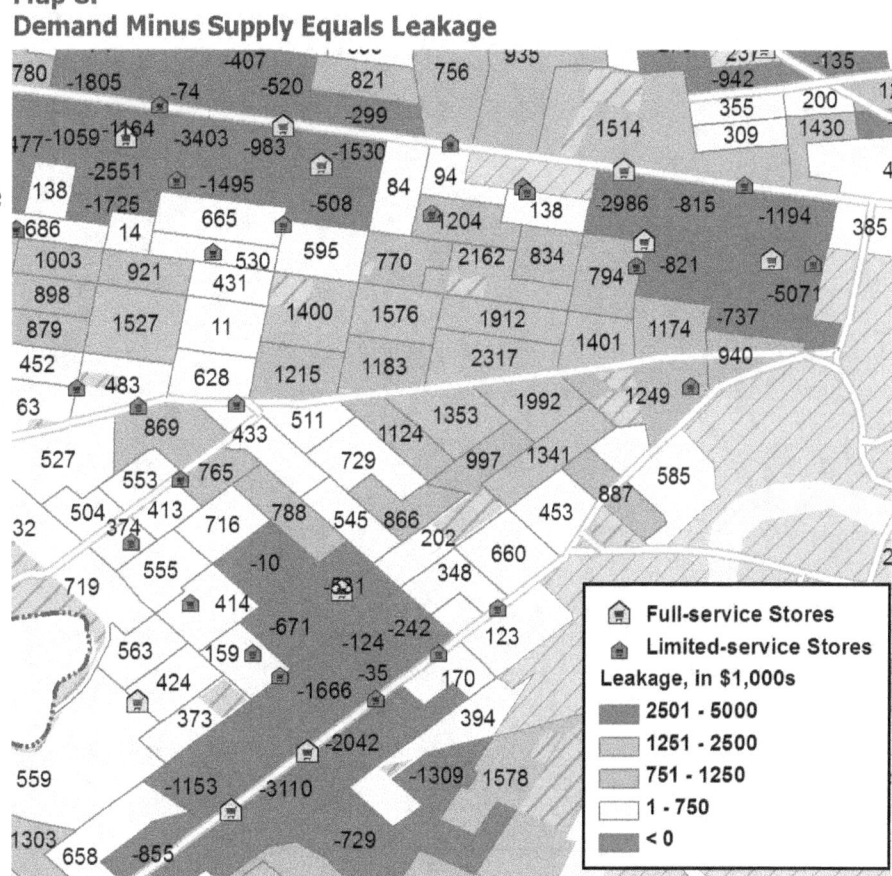

Section IV: Results

Approximately 24.6 million people, or 8% of the continental U.S. population, live in LSA areas. Of these 24.6 million residents, 46% (11,231,190) live in block groups with median household incomes at or below 80% of their metro or non-metro area median income. In the continental United States, by comparison, 29% (87.9 million residents) live in block groups within this income category. Therefore, a disproportionate number of residents living in LSA areas are low income. In total, TRF found 1,519 LSA areas representing 18,630 block groups in every state within our study area and in the District of Columbia.

TRF analyzed LSA areas at various levels of geography, including the U.S. census categories for core-based statistical areas, states and cities of various sizes. We also evaluated LSA areas by looking at the racial, ethnic and age composition of block groups within LSA areas. Lastly, we analyzed the economic-development opportunities these areas may represent through demand, leakage and overlap with areas eligible for the New Markets Tax Credit program and the 2011 Community Development Block Grant program.

Results by geography

There are many ways to determine where the problem is most pronounced for communities and thus where investment seems justifiable. The CDFI Fund's program guidelines prioritize distressed markets, which typically have a higher concentration of low-income residents. By targeting investments to low-income areas, programs can encourage investment activity in areas of greater distress—investment activity that might not occur without incentives. And the CDFI Fund is hardly alone in its focus; many federal, state and local investment programs target resources to distressed areas. Thus TRF presents the LSA results in ways that highlight LSA areas with the highest percentages of people and the highest percentages of residents from low-income block groups living in LSA areas. This is one way to rank the results, but lending organizations and anyone else choosing to use the data can use other means to prioritize areas and can combine various factors in multiple combinations to establish rankings. As noted, TRF aggregated LSA-area results using the following two factors:

(1) *Percentage of total population living in LSA areas*: This variable measures the percentage of the total population of a defined place (e.g. a city, state or metro area) living in all LSA areas within the geography. The percentage is then compared to the total population in the metro or non-metro area. TRF displays the results for each place.

(2) *Percentage of LSA area population living in low-income block groups*: This variable measures the extent to which the LSA problem is located in low-income areas. It calculates the percentage of LSA-area population living in block groups for which the median household income is at or below 80% of the AMI. It highlights where the LSA burden is felt more strongly in low-income areas. In each table, this column heading is noted as the "low-income burden."[57]

After places are scored based on these variables, TRF computes the average score for the place based on the two factors together and provides a composite ranking for each area. For simplicity, each factor is weighted equally.

Results at the national level

The LSA areas for the nation identified through TRF's analysis are displayed using the U.S. census's core-based statistical area (CBSA) designations: Major Metropolitan (population 1 million or more), Other Metropolitan (between 50,000 and 1 million), Micropolitan (urban cluster between 10,000 and 50,000 people), and Rural (which refers to rural areas that are not members of a metropolitan or a micropolitan area). Results can be seen in Table 5. Two observations stand out as particularly notable:

- The percentages of the populations in Major Metro, Other Metro and Rural areas living in LSA areas are 8.5%, 8.1% and 7.5% respectively and are relatively close to the national average of 8%. The percentage of residents in LSA areas from Micropolitan areas (5.9%) is notably lower than in the other three categories.

- Residents of metropolitan LSA areas (represented in Table 5 as both "major" and "other") are more likely to live in low-income areas than residents of micropolitan or rural LSA areas. While 30% of major metropolitan area residents are from low-income block groups, 49% of the LSA-area population lives in low-income block groups. Percentages for "other metro" are similar, with 27% of the residents in low-income block groups and 46.4% of LSA-area residents designated as low income.

Table 5:
National Results of LSA Areas by Census Core-Based Statistical Area Designations

Metro Area Category	Total Population	LSA Population	% of Total Pop in LSA	% of Total Pop in Low-Income Area	% of LSA Pop in Low-Income Area
Major Metro	164,805,874	13,930,574	8.5%	30.3%	49.0%
Micropolitan	30,889,982	1,828,723	5.9%	22.5%	24.9%
Other Metro	91,459,283	7,420,428	8.1%	27.1%	46.4%
Rural	19,512,549	1,458,038	7.5%	32.8%	34.6%
Nation	306,667,688	24,637,764	8.0%	28.7%	45.6%

See Appendix 3 for complete table.

Results at the state level

The average state has 8.6% of its population living in LSA areas, 42% of whom live in low-income census block groups. Table 6 lists the top 10 states plus the District of Columbia based on their composite ranking in terms of relative size of population with inadequate access and low-income burden. For a full listing of states and census places with their LSA characteristics, see Appendix 3.

- When the District of Columbia is included in the state ranking, it is first in both the total percentage of the population living in an LSA area, with 24%, and the total percentage of LSA- area residents living in low-income block groups, with 91%.
- Pennsylvania ranks second, with 12% of its residents living in LSA areas and 54% of these living in low-income block groups.

- Rhode Island is third, with 14% of its residents living in LSA areas and 53% of those residents living in low-income block groups.
- The remaining top 10 states tend to rank significantly higher in one variable than the other.

We share state rankings with caution, as the differences among their composite rankings reflect not only the equity or inequity of access but also the degree to which that inequity impacts lower-income areas disproportionately. This composite ranking is offered only as a summary measure, and we strongly recommend that practitioners and policymakers consider the contribution of each factor to the overall score. States differ greatly in size, income levels, spatial segregation of households by income and food retail accessibility. Each of these factors plays heavily into crafting appropriate interventions. (See Table 6, LSA Figures by State.)

Table 6:
LSA Figures by State

Geography	Total Population	Population in LSA	Composite Rank
District of Columbia	601,722	143,167	
Pennsylvania	12,698,826	1,528,284	1
Rhode Island	1,052,729	148,745	2
Louisiana	4,532,703	694,257	3
Connecticut	3,572,522	273,595	4
Illinois	12,827,020	1,048,199	5
Ohio	11,534,079	939,126	6
West Virginia	1,852,161	309,237	7
Tennessee	6,344,653	449,129	8
New York	19,375,996	1,459,034	9
Maryland	5,773,198	602,845	10

See Appendix 3 for complete table.

Results for cities and towns

TRF analyzed census places (such as cities and towns) to determine their ranking compared to other locations within the categories. This process grouped census places into subcategories based on total population. The analysis was performed using the two variables noted above. When areas have identical composite scores, the area with the larger population living in an LSA area is given the higher composite rank.

The Top 10 cities indicates those cities in this population range where the problem is most pronounced.

Cities with populations greater than 500,000:
There are 33 cities in the continental United States in this category. On average, 13% of large-city populations live in LSA areas, with 65% of them living in low-income block groups. Table 7 lists the top 10 cities in this population group based on their composite rankings of relative population size and low-income burden.

- Washington, D.C. ranks first overall, with 24% of its population living in LSA areas and 91% of the LSA population living in low-income block groups.
- Baltimore is second, with 30% of the population living in LSA areas and 86% of its LSA residents living in low-income block groups.
- Philadelphia is third, with 21% of the population living in LSA areas, of whom 85% are living in low-income block groups.
- The remaining top 10 large cities are mostly older, industrial areas in the Midwest, Northeast, and South.

Table 7:
LSA Figures for Top 10 Cities with Populations of More Than 500,000

Geography	Total Population	Population in LSA	% of Pop in LSA	% of LSA Pop in Low-Income Area	Composite Rank
Washington, D.C.	601,722	143,167	24%	91%	1
Baltimore, MD	620,956	184,075	30%	86%	2
Philadelphia, PA	1,525,931	324,927	21%	85%	3
Dallas, TX	1,222,935	203,339	17%	87%	4
Milwaukee, WI	594,651	136,412	23%	81%	5
Detroit, MI	713,753	165,492	23%	75%	6
Memphis, TN	646,247	134,632	21%	82%	7
Boston, MA	616,850	152,765	25%	61%	8
Nashville, TN	598,704	56,155	9%	90%	9
Louisville, KY	607,255	45,326	7%	95%	10

See Appendix 3 for complete table.

Cities with populations between 250,000 and 500,000: The average city of this size has 16% of its population living in LSA areas. Of those living in LSA areas, 68% are in low-income block groups. Thirty-four cities fall within this population range. Table 8 lists the top 10 cities in this group based on their composite rankings of relative population size and low-income burden.

- Cleveland ranks first overall, with a relative LSA-area population size of 22%; 93% of its LSA residents live in low-income block groups, and this percentage is also described as its low-income burden.

- Kansas City ranks second, with 9% of the total population living in LSA areas. Of those living in LSA areas, 97% live in low-income block groups.
- St. Louis ranks third, with 41% of the population living in LSA areas, of whom 78% live in low-income block groups.
- The relative size of St. Louis's LSA problem is over four times that of Kansas City (41% vs. 9%). However, Kansas City's low-income burden is significantly higher than St. Louis's (97% vs. 78%), resulting in nearly identical composite rankings.[58]
- The remaining top 10 medium-sized cities are mostly older, industrial areas in the Midwest and Northeast.

Table 8:
LSA Figures for Top 10 Cities with Populations Between 250,000 and 500,000

Geography	Total Population	Population in LSA	% of Pop in LSA	% of LSA Pop in Low-Income Area	Composite Rank
Cleveland, OH	396,845	88,272	22%	93%	1
Kansas City, MO	459,733	41,009	9%	97%	2
St. Louis, MO	318,905	130,200	41%	78%	3
Newark, NJ	276,609	34,807	13%	95%	4
Buffalo, NY	261,369	93,680	36%	77%	5
Tulsa, OK	388,667	42,289	11%	89%	6
Bakersfield, CA	313,314	26,705	9%	97%	7
Pittsburgh, PA	305,965	145,245	47%	71%	8
Cincinnati, OH	301,177	137,516	46%	72%	9
St. Paul, MN	285,087	49,198	17%	79%	10

See Appendix 3 for complete table.

Cities with populations between 100,000 and 250,000: The average city in this category has 14% of its population living in LSA areas. Of those living in LSA areas, 63% live in low-income block groups. Nationally, 113 cities fall within this population range. Table 9 lists the top 10 cities in this population group based on their composite rankings of relative population size and low-income burden.

- Richmond, VA ranks first overall, with a relative LSA-area population of 44% and a low-income burden of 86%.
- Knoxville, TN ranks second, with 18% of the population living in LSA areas, of whom 100% live in low-income block groups.
- Syracuse, NY ranks third, with 26% of the total population living in LSA areas and 91% of the LSA-area population living in low-income block groups. These figures are notably high in both variables and suggest that not only does a significant portion of the population live in LSA areas, but that low-income block groups constitute a dramatic percentage of the LSA area.
- The remaining top 10 cities in this group are mostly older, industrial areas in the South and Northeast.

Table 9:
LSA Figures for Top 10 Cities with Populations Between 100,000 and 250,000

Geography	Total Population	Population in LSA	% of Pop in LSA	% of LSA Pop in Low-Income Area	Composite Rank
Richmond, VA	204,209	90,593	44%	86%	1
Knoxville, TN	178,493	31,637	18%	100%	2
Syracuse, NY	145,045	37,079	26%	91%	3
Baton Rouge, LA	210,687	62,715	30%	85%	4
New Haven, CT	129,763	64,460	50%	82%	5
Rochester, NY	210,480	78,369	37%	82%	6
Des Moines, IA	199,342	30,130	15%	100%	7
Hartford, CT	124,365	33,984	27%	86%	8
Savannah, GA	137,117	37,041	27%	85%	9
North Charleston, SC	117,472	24,287	21%	90%	10

See Appendix 3 for complete table.

Cities with populations between 50,000 and 100,000: There are 182 cities in this population category. The average has 17% of its population living in LSA areas, 51% of whom live in low-income areas. Table 10 lists the top 10 cities in this population group based on their composite rankings of relative population size and low-income burden.

- Camden, NJ ranks first overall, with a relative LSA population size of 29% and a low-income burden of 100%.
- Trenton, NJ and Gary, IN rank second and third, with 45% and 42% respectively of population living in LSA areas. Of those living in LSA areas, 91% in Trenton and 85% in Gary live in low-income block groups.
- The remaining top 10 cities in this group are mostly older, industrial areas in the Midwest and Northeast.

Table 10:
LSA Figures for Top 10 Cities with Populations Between 50,000 and 100,000

Geography	Total Population	Population in LSA	% of Pop in LSA	% of LSA Pop in Low-Income Area	Composite Rank
Camden, NJ	77,704	22,737	29%	100%	1
Trenton, NJ	84,891	38,466	45%	91%	2
Gary, IN	80,279	33,562	42%	85%	3
Lawrence, MA	76,412	29,252	38%	90%	4
Youngstown, OH	66,862	22,931	34%	93%	5
Waukegan, IL	87,742	41,928	48%	84%	6
Albany, NY	97,785	46,878	48%	83%	7
Schenectady, NY	66,499	34,557	52%	80%	8
Daytona Beach, Fl	53,916	17,210	32%	87%	9
Decatur, IL	64,508	17,301	27%	95%	10

See Appendix 3 for complete table.

Cities with populations less than 50,000: There are 1,467 cities in this category. The average has 17% of its population living in LSA areas, 51% of whom live in low-income block groups. However, because so many cities in this population group are entirely encompassed by LSA areas, we only include the first 10. Table 11.A shows 10 places in this population group with 100% values for both relative population size and low-income burden, in descending order by total population in the LSA area. Table 11.B and Table 11.C show the middle 10 cities representing areas with average LSA scopes in their area. The bottom cities represent the places where there is not an access problem. We provide these 10 places to give the reader a better understanding of why these much smaller places are more difficult to analyze. The middle 10 places show more realistic values for relative size and income burden because they are not entirely encompassed by LSA areas, while the bottom 10 places are extremely small (with less than 600 residents) and have 100% of their population in an LSA area, with none living in a low-income block group.

Table 11A:
LSA Figures for Top 10 Cities
with Populations Less Than 50,000

Geography	Total Population	Population in LSA	% of Pop in LSA	% of LSA Pop in Low-Income Area	Composite Rank
Holiday-Berkeley, NJ	12,710	12,710	100%	100%	1
Kings Point, FL	8,288	8,288	100%	100%	2
Abram-Perezville, TX	7,910	7,910	100%	100%	3
Ambridge, PA	7,067	7,067	100%	100%	4
Leisure, NJ	6,612	6,612	100%	100%	5
Century, FL	6,534	6,534	100%	100%	6
South Highpoint, FL	6,348	6,348	100%	100%	7
Earlimart, CA	5,828	5,828	100%	100%	8
South Bay, FL	5,424	5,424	100%	100%	9
Frostburg, MD	5,340	5,340	100%	100%	10

See Appendix 3 for complete table.

Table 11B:
LSA Figures for Middle 10 Cities
with Populations Less Than 50,000

Geography	Total Population	Population in LSA	% of Pop in LSA	% of LSA Pop in Low-Income Area
Bristol, RI	22,985	11,391	50%	16%
North St. Paul, MN	11,618	6,183	53%	10%
Lehi, UT	47,796	23,948	50%	14%
Falcon Heights, MN	5,321	1,927	36%	41%
Socorro, TX	28,220	12,069	43%	26%
Security-Widefield, CO	29,524	14,472	49%	12%
DeKalb, IL	35,504	4,364	12%	84%
Belleville, IL	41,377	12,522	30%	50%
Carteret, NJ	22,802	7,626	33%	43%
Drexel Heights, AZ	30,421	13,849	46%	16%

See Appendix 3 for complete table.

Table 11C:
LSA Figures for Bottom 10 Cities
with Populations Less Than 50,000

Geography	Total Population	Population in LSA	% of Pop in LSA	% of LSA Pop in Low-Income Area
Groton Long Point, CT	518	518	100%	0%
Arcadia, OK	508	508	100%	0%
Medicine Park, OK	491	491	100%	0%
Rosslyn Farms, PA	486	486	100%	0%
Morgan, TX	475	475	100%	0%
Arthur, NE	460	460	100%	0%
Westhope, ND	446	446	100%	0%
Mapleton, PA	442	442	100%	0%
Thomaston, ME	399	399	100%	0%
Hinton, OK	358	358	100%	0%

See Appendix 3 for complete table.

Metropolitan and micropolitan areas

The metropolitan and micropolitan areas (collectively known as Core-Based Statistical Areas, or CBSAs) listed below are each comprised of a core area with a substantial population and of adjacent communities (suburban counties, cities and towns) that are highly integrated socially and economically with that core.[59] Each metropolitan statistical area has at least one core urbanized area of 50,000 or more inhabitants, while each micropolitan statistical area has at least one core urban cluster of at least 10,000 but less than 50,000 inhabitants. This study analyzes results separately for core cities and entire CBSAs because core cities are expected to exhibit different characteristics than their respective metropolitan or micropolitan areas. Additionally, some readers may be more concerned with food access at one population level or another. LSA-area results can be customized for any geography, but the geographies presented in this paper are both relevant and broad in scope.

Major metropolitan areas (populations greater than 1 million):

The average major metropolitan area has 9% of its population living in LSA areas. Of those in LSA areas, 52% live in low-income block groups. Table 12 lists the top 10 major metro areas based on their composite rankings of relative population size and low-income burden.

- The Memphis metro area ranks first overall, with a relative LSA-area population of 12% and a low-income burden of 75%.
- The Pittsburgh and Richmond metro areas show the same composite ranking score. Yet the size of Pittsburgh's LSA problem is nearly twice that of Richmond's (18% vs. 10%), and Richmond's low-income burden is dramatically higher than Pittsburgh's (84% vs. 57%). These cities serve as examples of how there are various ways to prioritize and rank LSA areas. Ranked places may achieve their placement through different ways, signaling opportunities for different intervention strategies.
- The remaining top 10 major metro areas are largely older, industrial areas in the Midwest and Northeast, with the exception of New Orleans.

Table 12:
LSA Figures for Major Metro Areas with Populations Greater Than 1,000,000

Geography	Total Population	Population in LSA	% of Pop in LSA	% of LSA Pop in Low-Income Area	Composite Rank
Memphis, TN-MS-AR	1,315,850	155,419	12%	75%	1
Pittsburgh, PA	2,355,231	422,513	18%	57%	2
Richmond, VA	1,257,997	124,662	10%	84%	3
New Orleans-Metairie-Kenner, LA	1,167,694	242,172	21%	56%	4
Philadelphia-Camden-Wilmington, PA-NJ-DE-MD	5,964,299	796,746	13%	57%	5
Milwaukee-Waukesha-West Allis, WI	1,555,512	167,167	11%	71%	6
St. Louis, MO-IL	2,836,702	383,039	14%	50%	7
Baltimore-Towson, MD	2,710,302	350,267	13%	55%	8
Cleveland-Elyria-Mentor, OH	2,076,526	206,908	10%	61%	9
Buffalo-Niagara Falls, NY	1,135,409	210,555	19%	46%	10

See Appendix 3 for complete table.

Metropolitan areas with populations between 500,000 and 1 million: The average metropolitan area in this population category has 9.5% of its residents living in LSA areas, 49% of whom live in low-income block groups. Table 13 lists the top 10 metro areas in this category based on their composite rankings of relative population size and low-income burden.

- The Albany metro area ranks first overall, with a relative LSA population size of 15% and a low-income burden of 65%.
- Baton Rouge, LA and New Haven, CT follow in the second and third spots.
- Overall, the top 10 in this category predominantly consist of metro areas in the Northeast and South.

Table 13:
LSA Figures for Metro Areas with Populations Between 500,000 and 1,000,000

Geography	Total Population	Population in LSA	% of Pop in LSA	% of LSA Pop in Low-Income Area	Composite Rank
Albany-Schenectady-Troy, NY	870,462	134,880	15%	65%	1
Baton Rouge, LA	802,302	86,095	11%	77%	2
New Haven-Milford, CT	862,229	115,382	13%	67%	3
Harrisburg-Carlisle, PA	549,353	96,668	18%	58%	4
Wichita, KS	623,024	60,649	10%	75%	5
Springfield, MA	692,755	112,803	16%	56%	6
Youngstown-Warren-Boardman, OH-PA	565,509	67,411	12%	58%	7
El Paso, TX	800,634	95,763	12%	57%	8
McAllen-Edinburg-Mission, TX	774,636	320,982	41%	45%	9
Greensboro-High Point, NC	723,683	48,113	7%	71%	10

See Appendix 3 for complete table.

Metropolitan areas with populations between 250,000 and 500,000: The average metropolitan area in this population range has 8.9% of its residents living in LSA areas. Of its LSA-area population, 47% live in low-income block groups. Table 14 lists the top 10 metro areas in this population group based on their composite rankings of relative population size and low-income burden.

- The Trenton, NJ metro area ranks first overall, with a relative LSA population size of 17% and a low-income burden of 70%, followed by Columbus, GA and Savannah, GA in the top three.
- Overall, the top 10 in this category is evenly distributed throughout metro areas in the Northeast, South, and Midwest.

Table 14:
LSA Figures for Metro Areas with Populations Between 250,000 and 500,000

Geography	Total Population	Population in LSA	% of Pop in LSA	% of LSA Pop in Low-Income Area	Composite Rank
Trenton-Ewing, NJ	366,608	62,535	17%	70%	1
Columbus, GA-AL	294,919	36,997	13%	73%	2
Savannah, GA	347,596	38,272	11%	83%	3
Erie, PA	280,523	34,465	12%	71%	4
Atlantic City, NJ	274,537	58,108	21%	57%	5
Lexington-Fayette, KY	472,040	53,010	11%	70%	6
Lansing-East Lansing, MI	464,028	64,196	14%	62%	7
Fort Wayne, IN	416,160	28,244	7%	94%	8
Hagerstown-Martinsburg, MD-WV	269,092	39,557	15%	59%	9
Ann Arbor, MI	344,783	65,925	19%	53%	10

See Appendix 3 for complete table.

Metropolitan areas with populations less than 250,000: The average metropolitan area with this population range has 9.6% of its residents living in LSA areas and a low-income burden of 38%. Table 15 lists the top 10 metro areas in this population group based on their composite rankings of relative population size and low-income burden.

- The Decatur, IL metro area ranks first overall, with a relative LSA population size of 18% and a low-income burden of 81%, followed by Muskegon-Norton Shores, MI and College Station-Bryan, TX, which rank second and third respectively.
- Overall, the top 10 in this category predominantly consist of metro areas in the South and Midwest.

Table 15:
LSA Figures for Metro Areas Populations Less Than 250,000

Geography	Total Population	Population in LSA	% of Pop in LSA	% of LSA Pop in Low-Income Area	Composite Rank
Decatur, IL	110,726	20,260	18%	81%	1
Muskegon-Norton Shores, MI	172,186	25,131	15%	85%	2
College Station-Bryan, TX	228,644	39,183	17%	61%	3
Lafayette, IN	201,731	31,146	15%	66%	4
Show Low, AZ	107,417	17,427	16%	63%	5
Racine, WI	195,337	31,253	16%	61%	6
Monroe, LA	176,384	45,279	26%	50%	7
Houma-Bayou Cane-Thibodaux, LA	208,158	57,119	27%	48%	8
Pueblo, CO	159,001	30,311	19%	51%	9
Sioux City, IA-NE-SD	143,521	29,835	21%	50%	10

See Appendix 3 for complete table.

Micropolitan areas: Micropolitan statistical areas tend to be much smaller than metropolitan areas and must have at least one urban cluster with between 10,000 and 50,000 residents. For all micropolitan areas with at least one LSA area, the population ranges in size from just over 12,000 (Tallulah, LA) to roughly 190,000 (Torrington, CT), with an average population of 59,324.

The average micropolitan area has 13% of its population living in LSAs, 24% of whom live in low-income block groups. Table 16 lists the top 10 micropolitan areas based on their composite rankings of relative size and low-income burden.

- The Amsterdam, NY micropolitan area ranks first overall, with a relative size of 36% and a low-income burden of 58%, followed by Macomb, IL and Clarksdale, MS in the top three.
- Overall, the top 10 are evenly distributed throughout the Northeast, Midwest, South and Southwest.

Table 16:
LSA Figures for Micropolitan Areas

Geography	Total Population	Population in LSA	% of Pop in LSA	% of LSA Pop in Low-Income Area	Composite Rank
Amsterdam, NY	50,215	18,152	36%	58%	1
Macomb, IL	32,604	8,045	25%	87%	2
Clarksdale, MS	26,140	9,216	35%	48%	3
Tallulah, LA	12,091	3,080	25%	69%	4
Gallup, NM	71,476	39,824	56%	40%	5
Marion, OH	66,490	17,266	26%	55%	6
Ottumwa, IA	35,611	8,117	23%	59%	7
Sierra Vista-Douglas, AZ	131,299	30,887	24%	54%	8
Price, UT	21,396	7,548	35%	39%	9
New Castle, PA	91,095	24,911	27%	43%	10

See Appendix 3 for complete table.

As noted above, TRF analyzed LSA areas based on income and population size. Depending on a specific program's goals and overall mission, there are numerous ways to prioritize areas based on their need for additional grocery retail. Some programs might focus exclusively on geographies in which low access is concentrated in low-income areas, while others might be more concerned with improving access in areas in which LSA-area residents constitute a significant percentage of the total population. Others might be more concerned with improving access for minority or elderly populations. PolicyMap allows users to analyze LSA areas overlaid with census data, USDA Food Desert locations and other relevant indicators.

Results by race, ethnicity and income

TRF examined whether there was a greater likelihood of living in an LSA area if one is of a particular race, ethnicity, income level or age. We further evaluated whether the odds change based upon the population of a city. TRF reviewed the results at the national level and at census designations for places. Table 17 displays the results

of this analysis. The degree of equity or inequity within these groupings varies by the size of the city. In specific cities and neighborhoods across the country, persons of color are more likely to experience inequitable and disadvantageous supermarket access than people who are White, non-Hispanic. Similarly, people of lower income experience inequitable access when compared to people of higher income. These data do not appear to reveal remarkable trends with respect to age for either children (18 years of age or younger) or the elderly (over the age of 65).

The ratios shown in Table 17 are established so that a value of 1.0 indicates that the target group (such as people who are Black, non-Hispanic) has the same likelihood of living in an LSA area when viewed against its comparison group (such as people who are White, non-Hispanic). Values of greater than 1.0 indicate a disadvantage for the target group; values of less than 1.0 show an advantage. The first column of Table 17 shows the likelihood that people of a particular race, ethnicity, income level or age live in an LSA area.

Table 17:
Likelihood of Living in an LSA Area by Race, Ethnicity, Age and City Size

The likelihood of living in an LSA area	Continental U.S.	Cities with populations greater than 500,000	Cities with populations between 250,000 and 500,000	Cities with populations between 100,000 and 250,000	Cities with populations between 50,000 and 100,000	Cities with populations less than 50,000
if you are Black, non-Hispanic compared to White, non-Hispanic	2.49	2.97	3.86	2.55	1.93	1.08
if you are Hispanic compared to White, non-Hispanic	1.38	1.50	.96	1.52	1.23	1.27
if you live in low-income area compared to non-low-income area	2.28	2.68	3.19	2.92	1.89	1.71
if you are under age 18 compared to over age 18	1.06	1.18	.99	1.07	1.09	1.07
if you are over age 65 compared to under 65	.91	.88	.96	.89	.88	.98

In the continental United States, a person is 2.49 times more likely to live in an LSA area if that person is Black, non-Hispanic than if the person is White, non-Hispanic. The results also show that if someone is Black, non-Hispanic, the likelihood of living in an LSA area increases in a city with a population over 100,000. The highest risk is for those who are Black, non-Hispanic and who live in cities with a population between 250,000 and 500,000. This population is 3.86 times more likely to live in an LSA area than a White, non-Hispanic person living in a city of the same size.

Across the continental United States, a person who is Hispanic is 1.38 times more likely to live in an LSA area than a person who is White, non-Hispanic. The inequity is greatest in the largest cities (with more than 500,000 people) and modest-sized cities (100,000 to 250,000). There is, however, no inequity (.96) between Hispanics and non-Hispanics in cities with populations between 250,000 and 500,000.

In general, a person living in a low-income block group (a block group with a median household income at or below 80% of area median income) is 2.28 times more likely to live in an LSA area than a person living in a non-low-income block group. The inequity shown by these ratios is substantial, and it is greatest in the larger cities. For example, residents of low-income areas are more than three times more likely to have inequitable and disadvantageous access than residents of higher-income areas in cities with between 250,000 and 500,000 residents.

Nationwide, an individual under age 18 is 1.06 times more likely to live in an LSA area than an individual aged 18 or over. This disadvantage is not substantial, so we can conclude that, in general, children are not at a substantially higher risk of inequitable and disadvantageous food access when compared to people who are over 18. Where a difference exists, it is most pronounced among children living in the largest cities, where the ratio is 1.18 times.

Nationwide and in all city sizes, being over age 65 does not show an increased likelihood of inequitable and disadvantageous access to food retail; the ratio is less than 1. In fact, the data show that individuals over age 65 have slightly less risk of being in an LSA area than the people under the age of 65.

Results by estimated leakage

Understanding the economic landscape within a given LSA area is important because this knowledge can help determine viable strategies for increasing access. The most important market indicator from a retail-industry perspective is the unmet or inadequately met local demand for food, which is known as leakage. Leakage in financial terms represents "a measure of retail sales lost by a community to a competitive market, indicating the need for more retail development in an area." [60] Sales "leaked out" of an area represent the unmet demand for food in a community. So a leakage figure captures the current amount of food that residents of an area purchase at another location. To calculate leakage, two amounts must be known: the existing amount of food that residents of the area purchase, and the total food sales occurring within the study area. If the total demand for food exceeds the total sales from stores, the difference in food sales is "leaked out." Leakage is presumed to result in a loss of economic activity, jobs and perhaps tax revenue for the community (if the lost sales occur outside of their local taxing jurisdiction).

Different methods are used to estimate both general retail leakage and leakage broken down by sectors (such as grocery leakage). In this analysis, TRF estimates sales using data from the U.S. Bureau of Labor Statistics' Consumer Expenditure Survey. The Consumer Expenditure Survey collects information on the purchasing habits of households in different income categories and by region of the country. These estimates of potential spending by income level and region are then multiplied by household counts to calculate demand within the area. Since leakage measurements assign a dollar amount to unmet demand, they can suggest the scale of new retail needed to satisfy local demand.

The estimated level of leakage provides a way to distinguish between LSA areas that could support a new full-service supermarket and those areas in which other forms of food retail may prove more viable and sustainable. For those areas that can support a new full-service supermarket, the potential economic benefits that a store can bring to the communities serve as a strong incentive for intervention. This study identifies LSA areas that may have the market potential to support a new full-service supermarket.

Categorizing LSA areas by leakage estimates

Leakage estimates can help define the parameters for proposed interventions. The leakage results fall into four general ranges, each associated with a different strategy for reducing leakage:

(1)   LSA areas with **less than $6 million** in estimated unmet demand are areas in which the most appropriate strategy can be either to upgrade existing stores or to introduce alternative approaches, such as farmers' markets, a store delivery program or improved transportation to an existing store. (TRF's analysis shows 346 LSA areas within this range.)

(2)   LSA areas with unmet demand of **between $6 million and $12 million** are areas with sizable demand but in which a small store or an investment into an existing store may be a more appropriate and viable strategy. (There are 426 LSA areas within this range.)

(3)   LSA areas with leakage of **between $12 million and $24 million** can support a full-service supermarket. (There are 419 LSA areas within this range.)

(4)   LSA areas with leakage of **more than $24 million** may need more than one full-service supermarket to meet demand. (There are 328 LSA areas within this range.)

Table 18 displays the number and percentage of LSA areas in the nation by estimated leakage. They are distributed relatively equally across the four categories, and 74% appear to be able to support a supermarket intervention, which could mean either investment in a new store or the expansion of an existing store.

Table 18:
LSA Areas in the U.S. by Leakage Categories

	Up to $6 million	$6 million to $12 million	$12 million to $24 million	More than $24 million
# of LSA areas	346	426	419	328
% of all LSA areas	23%	28%	28%	22%

Utlizing economic resources for supporting development in LSA areas

Many LSA areas fall within low-income census tracts, making them more likely to be able to utilize federal incentives to subsidize development costs. Of the 1,519 LSA areas, 80% are within 2011 Census tracts eligible for Community Development Block Grants (CDBGs) and 60% are within areas eligible for the New Markets Tax Credit (NMTC). Both CDBG and NMTC provide significant resources that could be targeted to support interventions. It is likely that other state, local and federal economic-development programs may also be available to support the financing of new stores.

Identifying existing shopping options in LSA areas

Many LSA areas have some food stores within their boundaries. The food option may be a small grocery store, a chain drug store and, rarely, a full-service store or a limited assortment store. Most LSA areas have demand in excess of what is captured by existing stores. The excess demand may indicate that the existing stores have limited selections or that they are inaccessible to area residents; either way, residents are shopping elsewhere to meet their food needs. Leakage information, combined with local market knowledge and in-store observations, can help determine if existing stores are potential investment opportunities for a CDFI working to expand access.

Nationally, 67% of LSA areas—1,024 areas—contain a store within their boundaries. All LSA areas are likely to have some stores within their boundaries, as noted in the table below. LSA areas with leakage equal to or greater than $24 million are most likely to have an existing store within their boundaries; 88% of these LSA areas have a store. Table 19 shows LSA areas with an existing small grocery store or drug store within their boundaries.

Table 19:
LSA Areas with an Existing Store in Their Boundaries

	Up to $6 million	$6 million to $12 million	$12 million to $24 million	More than $24 million
# LSA areas	346	426	419	328
# of LSA areas with an existing store	189	256	292	287
% of LSA areas with an existing store	55%	60%	70%	88%

Results in spatial format

In both urban and rural areas, a single LSA area may cover a vast contiguous geographic territory that extends beyond a city, county or state boundary. For this reason, viewing the LSA areas spatially allows users to assess the appropriateness of an intervention strategy. Large LSA areas may represent multiple rather than single market opportunities. For example, Map 9 shows that in Knox County, NE, LSA1 contains 99 block groups with a total leakage in excess of $60 million annually. The LSA area extends more than 250 miles from its northern to its southern boundary. Even if a store were placed in the center of the LSA area, it would not be likely to serve the vast number of residents at the northern and southern ends of the area. Furthermore, while $60 million is the aggregate leakage amount, it is so dispersed throughout the area that the solution in this area may be several small grocery stores rather than two large full-service stores. Thus, while we do associate an intervention strategy with a level of leakage, we recognize that each LSA area must be evaluated spatially and in concert with data on its local stores and population density to determine the most viable strategy for that area.

Map 9:
LSA Knox County, Nebraska 1

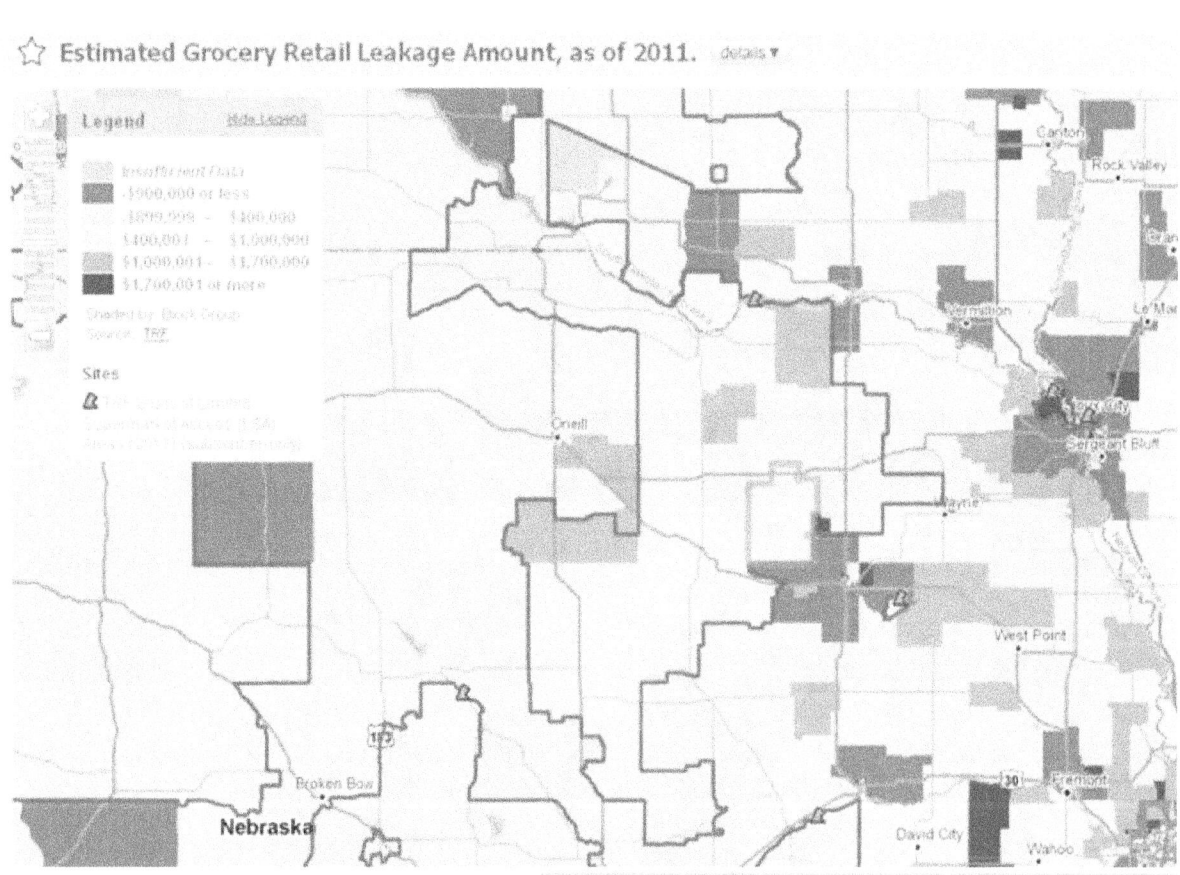

Estimated Grocery Retail Leakage Amount, as of 2011. details ▾

Limited Supermarket Access (LSA) Name: LSA Knox County, Nebraska 1
Population Weighted LSA Score: 57
Block Groups in LSA: 99
Est. Grocery Retail Leakage Amount: $60,200,000
Est. Grocery Retail Leakage Rate: 53%
Est. Total Grocery Retail Demand: $113,900,000
Est. Total Grocery Retail Sq Ft Demand: 200,000
Est. Grocery Retail Sq Ft Leaked: 106,000
Stores in LSA: 39
Population: 89,158

Keeping those caveats in mind, we prepared the following tables to present LSA-area leakage results for each state. The states are organized in tables by census divisions of the country. For each state, we provide the total number of LSA areas. These charts also display two characteristics of the state's LSA area results: the estimated leakage amount using the ranges noted above, and the number of LSA areas within the leakage category that have an existing store within their boundaries. If an LSA area extends over more than one state, each state is noted as having an LSA area, and the total leakage amount is allocated to each state. (See Tables 20 through 28.) For example, this first table shows results for states within the New England census division. It notes that TRF identified 46 LSA areas in Massachusetts.

These are the characteristics of the 46 LSA areas:

- 1 LSA area has an estimated leakage of less than $6 million, and it does not have any existing stores within its boundaries;
- 8 LSA areas have estimated leakages of between $6 million and $12 million, and 62% (5) of these have stores within the boundaries;
- 22 LSA areas have estimated leakages of between $12 million and $24 million, and of these 72% (15 LSA areas) have stores within their boundaries; and
- 15 LSA areas have an estimated leakage of above $24 million, and 100% of these have stores within their boundaries.

Generally, the information conveys the composition of LSA areas in each state. These tables do not rank states or control for population density.

Table 20:
LSA Results for States in New England Division

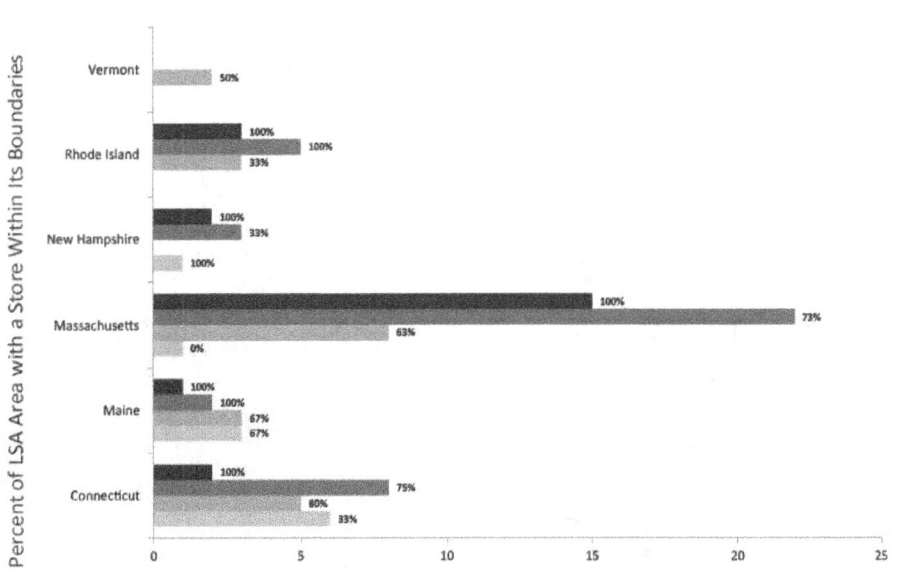

Table 21:
LSA Results for States in East South Central Division

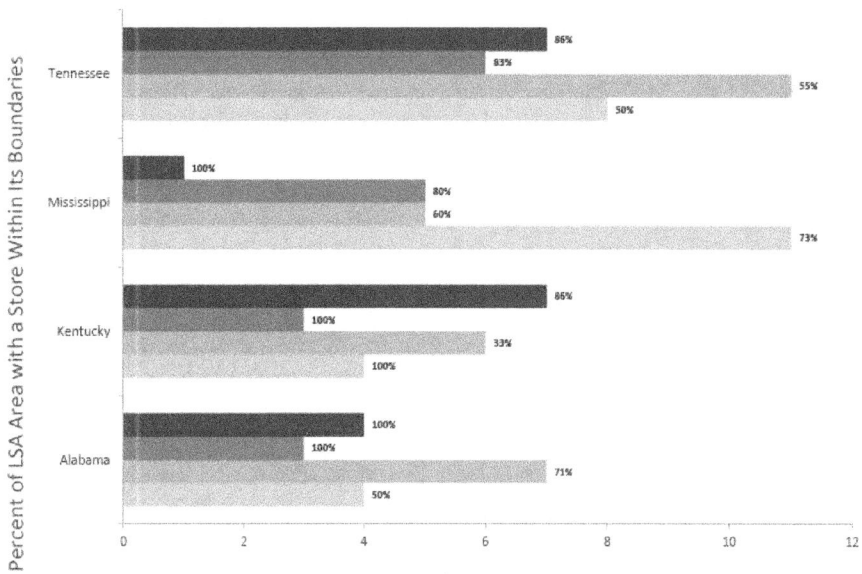

Total Number of LSA Areas by Leakage Categories

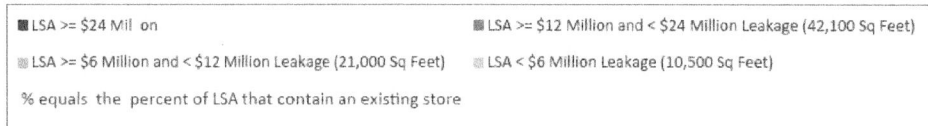

- ■ LSA >= $24 Mil on
- ■ LSA >= $12 Million and < $24 Million Leakage (42,100 Sq Feet)
- ▨ LSA >= $6 Million and < $12 Million Leakage (21,000 Sq Feet)
- ▨ LSA < $6 Million Leakage (10,500 Sq Feet)
- % equals the percent of LSA that contain an existing store

Table 22:
LSA Results for States in South Atlantic Division

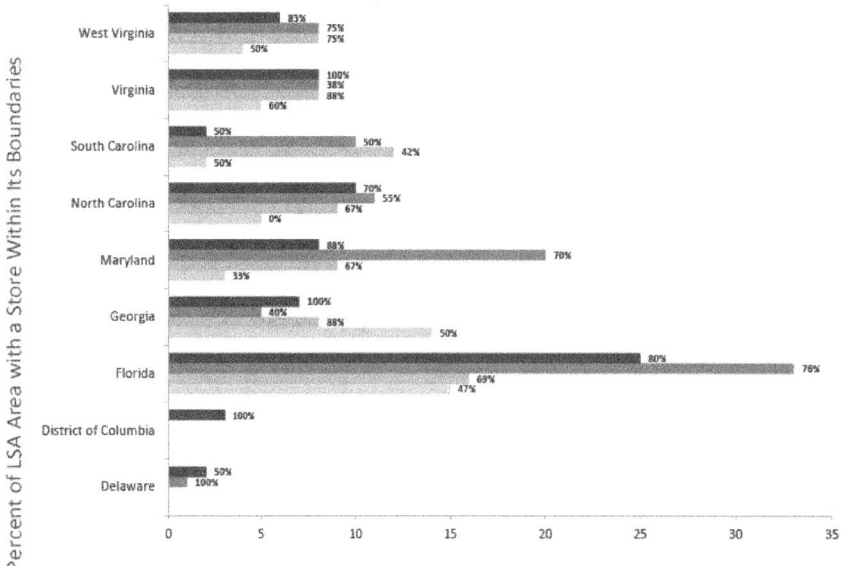

Total Number of LSA Areas by Leakage Categories

Table 23:
LSA Results for States in Mountain Division

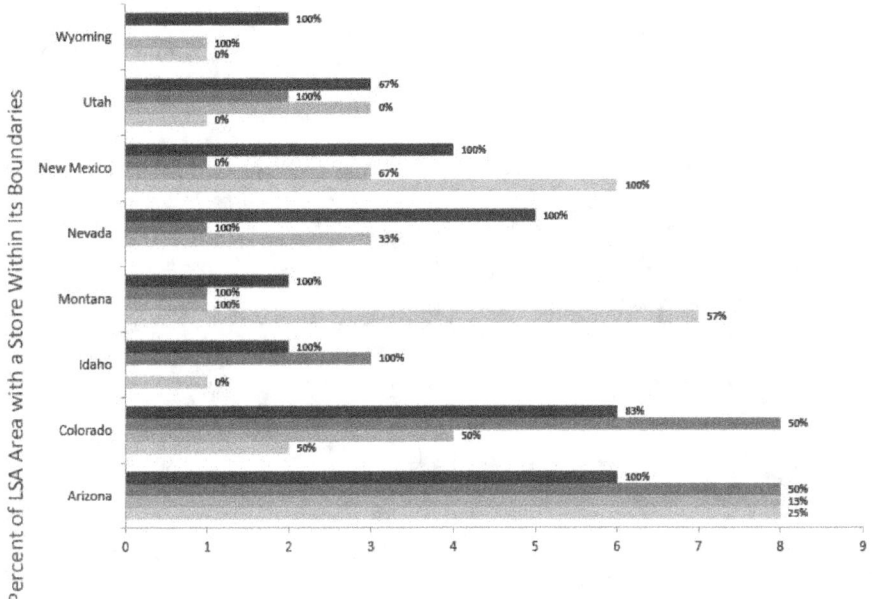

Percent of LSA Area with a Store Within Its Boundaries

Total Number of LSA Areas by Leakage Categories

■ LSA >= $24 Mil on	■ LSA >= $12 Million and < $24 Million Leakage (42,100 Sq Feet)
▨ LSA >= $6 Million and < $12 Million Leakage (21,000 Sq Feet)	▨ LSA < $6 Million Leakage (10,500 Sq Feet)
% equals the percent of LSA that contain an existing store	

Table 24:
LSA Results for States in Middle Atlantic Division

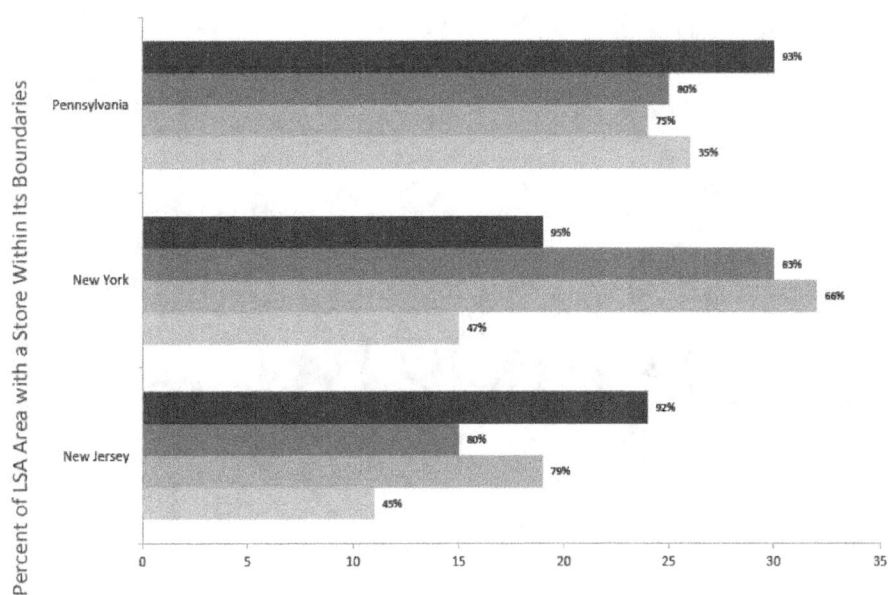

Percent of LSA Area with a Store Within Its Boundaries

Total Number of LSA Areas by Leakage Categories

Table 25:
LSA Results for States in West Northern Central Division

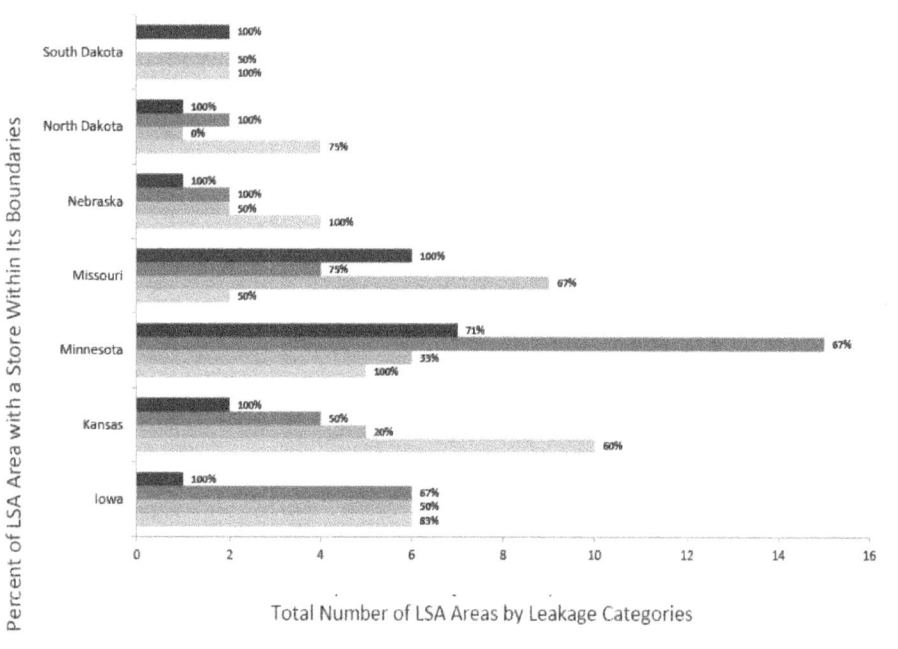

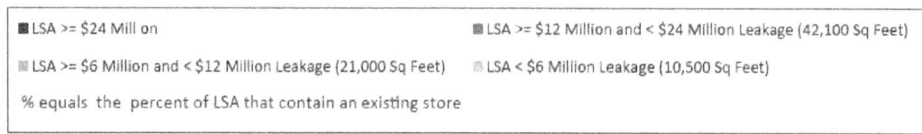

- LSA >= $24 Mill on
- LSA >= $12 Million and < $24 Million Leakage (42,100 Sq Feet)
- LSA >= $6 Million and < $12 Million Leakage (21,000 Sq Feet)
- LSA < $6 Million Leakage (10,500 Sq Feet)
- % equals the percent of LSA that contain an existing store

Table 26:
LSA Results for States in Pacific Division

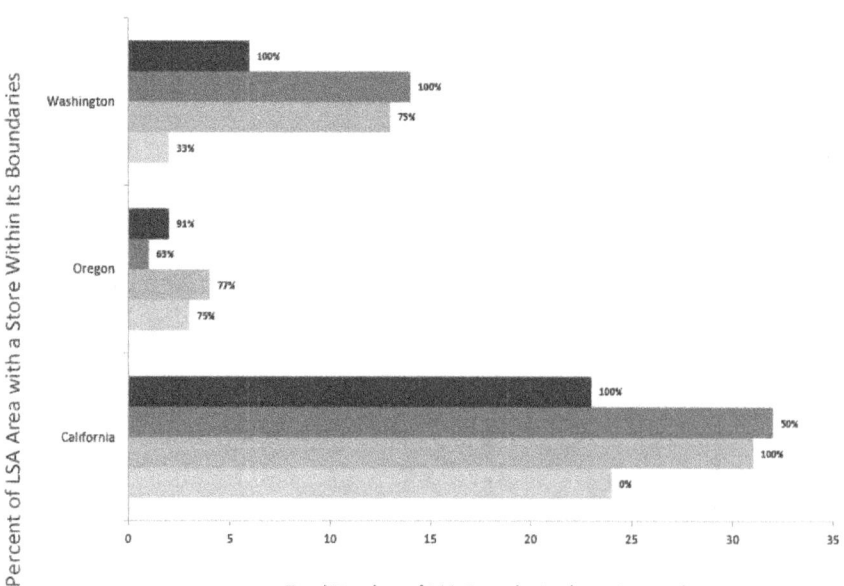

Table 27:
LSA Results for States in West South Central Division

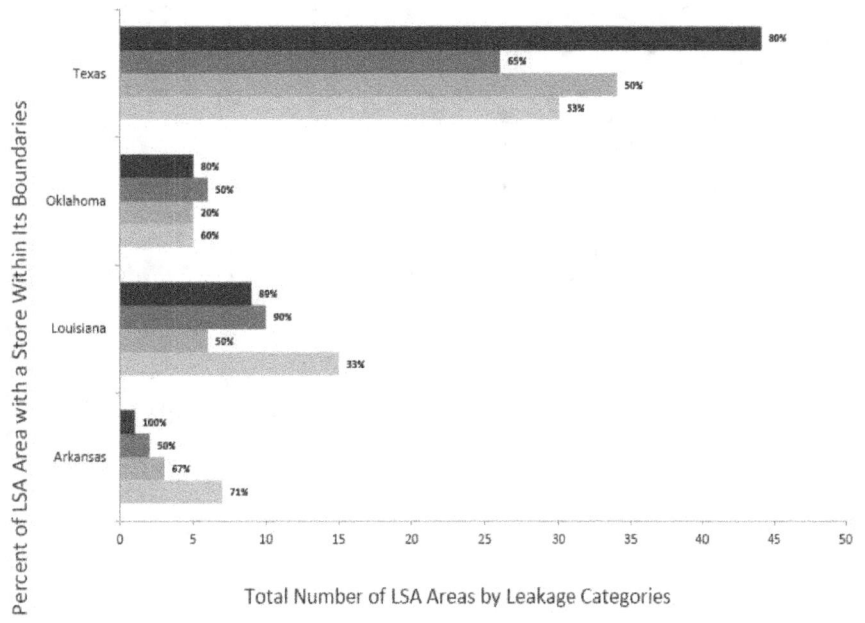

Percent of LSA Area with a Store Within Its Boundaries

Total Number of LSA Areas by Leakage Categories

- ■ LSA >= $24 Mill on
- ■ LSA >= $12 Million and < $24 Million Leakage (42,100 Sq Feet)
- ▥ LSA >= $6 Million and < $12 Million Leakage (21,000 Sq Feet)
- ▨ LSA < $6 Million Leakage (10,500 Sq Feet)
- % equals the percent of LSA that contain an existing store

Table 28:
LSA Results for States in East North Central Division

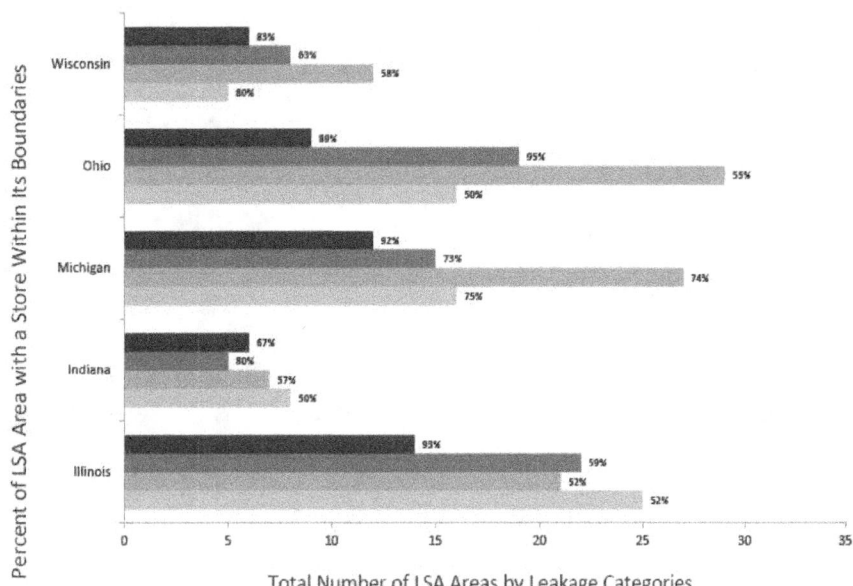

Percent of LSA Area with a Store Within Its Boundaries

Total Number of LSA Areas by Leakage Categories

In summary, residents living in LSA areas spend on average $1,120 annually on food products outside of their areas. In terms of per capita spending, leakage is highest in New Jersey, Maine, Colorado, Vermont and New Hampshire, where the average per-resident leakage is $1,441. Per capita leakage for the median five states, which include Mississippi, Missouri, Michigan, Kentucky and Illinois, is $1,112. Per capita leakage is lowest in North Dakota, South Dakota, Delaware, Nebraska and Montana at $698. It is important to weigh leakage data with information on the available shopping options. To allow users to understand the existing food landscape, store location information is also available on PolicyMap.

Conclusion

TRF designed this study to provide practitioners—developers, lenders and grocery store operators—with reliable, common standards for evaluating food access. Nationwide, practitioners can use this tool to identify and prioritize areas with the strongest need for supermarkets and to quantify demand for additional development. The results of this analysis are available down to the block group level on PolicyMap so that users can view this information in concert with other relevant social, demographic and economic data. Appendix 4 provides an application of the analysis, showing how a CDFI can use the data to prioritize the allocation of resources to LSA areas within its community.

Through this study, TRF hopes to enable practitioners to take the first steps in designing a financing program by establishing priority areas and evaluating investment opportunities. Two key metrics, access scores and grocery leakage estimates, can help practitioners prioritize LSA areas according to the characteristics most relevant from a programmatic perspective. The two metrics help characterize the degree to which an LSA area is underserved and its capacity to support additional food sales. This level of understanding can inform appropriate interventions.

While this is a study of supermarket access, not all LSA areas can support a full-service supermarket. As the administrator of the FFFI, TRF worked to increase community access to healthy, affordable food by financing new stores, existing stores and alternative programs, such as food cooperatives and farmers' markets. The leakage results for each LSA area provide a general framework for understanding the feasibility of supporting stores of various sizes and for determining whether the strategy should focus on new store development, existing store expansion or an alternative intervention. The study also offers a basis for focusing healthy-food-access intervention programs in very specific ways. For example, once an LSA area is identified, practitioners and local stakeholders can further refine a program's goals in terms of its target population or in terms of how it meets existing economic-development priorities. Here are some suggested next steps to consider when using the data for developing more strategic local interventions:

(1)   Evaluate the LSA areas based upon leakage, access score and existing shopping options within and around the LSA area. The framework for evaluation (Diagram 1) offers a way to think about all LSA areas within a community and to frame a discussion with stakeholders about where need exists and what type of intervention strategy is appropriate.

(2)   Determine local accessibility as it relates to specific categories of individuals. The results of TRF's methodology describe the relative accessibility or inaccessibility of spatial areas to supermarkets. However, some individuals living in well-served areas may nonetheless have limited access to food, such as the elderly or disabled (who often have diminished mobility) or individuals in an area with high car-ownership rates who do not have access to a vehicle. To determine specific needs of residents in a given location, local practitioners should supplement TRF's analysis with localized information.

(3)   Assess possible locations for stores. LSA areas highlight the concentration of need and don't represent a recommendation for the exact placement of a store. This study is not intended to be a criterion for the exclusion of properties or areas from program designs. Vacancy, zoning and current land uses are among the highly localized characteristics that go into determining where a new store can be built or an existing store can be

augmented to serve an LSA area. Locating a store within the core of an LSA area will likely serve the most residents in need, but sites to build upon may be too costly. In addition, TRF's assessment excludes census block groups with very low populations (nonresidential areas). If a nonresidential area is adjacent to the LSA area, however, it may offer the necessary parcel for a store. Thus there are many factors beyond the scope of TRF's methodology for a local assessment to consider, including public-transit access.

(4) Gaining access to healthy and affordable food is often a first step toward healthy eating habits. Low-income communities often experience inequitable access as well as high obesity rates and other high-risk health conditions. But improved access alone does not ensure healthy eating. If reducing obesity and improving health outcomes are goals, then resources allocated to support community education programs or other health initiatives focused on changing eating and shopping habits must work in tandem with increasing access.

TRF presents this study as a shared tool that can provide a common foundation for a national dialogue on limited healthy-food access. This research sets the stage for collaboration and provides an opportunity for practitioners to become more engaged in strategies to address inequitable access. Most importantly, with the data tools now available, local community stakeholders have a first step towards understanding and tackling issues of food-access disparity.

Diagram 1:
Framework for Evaluation

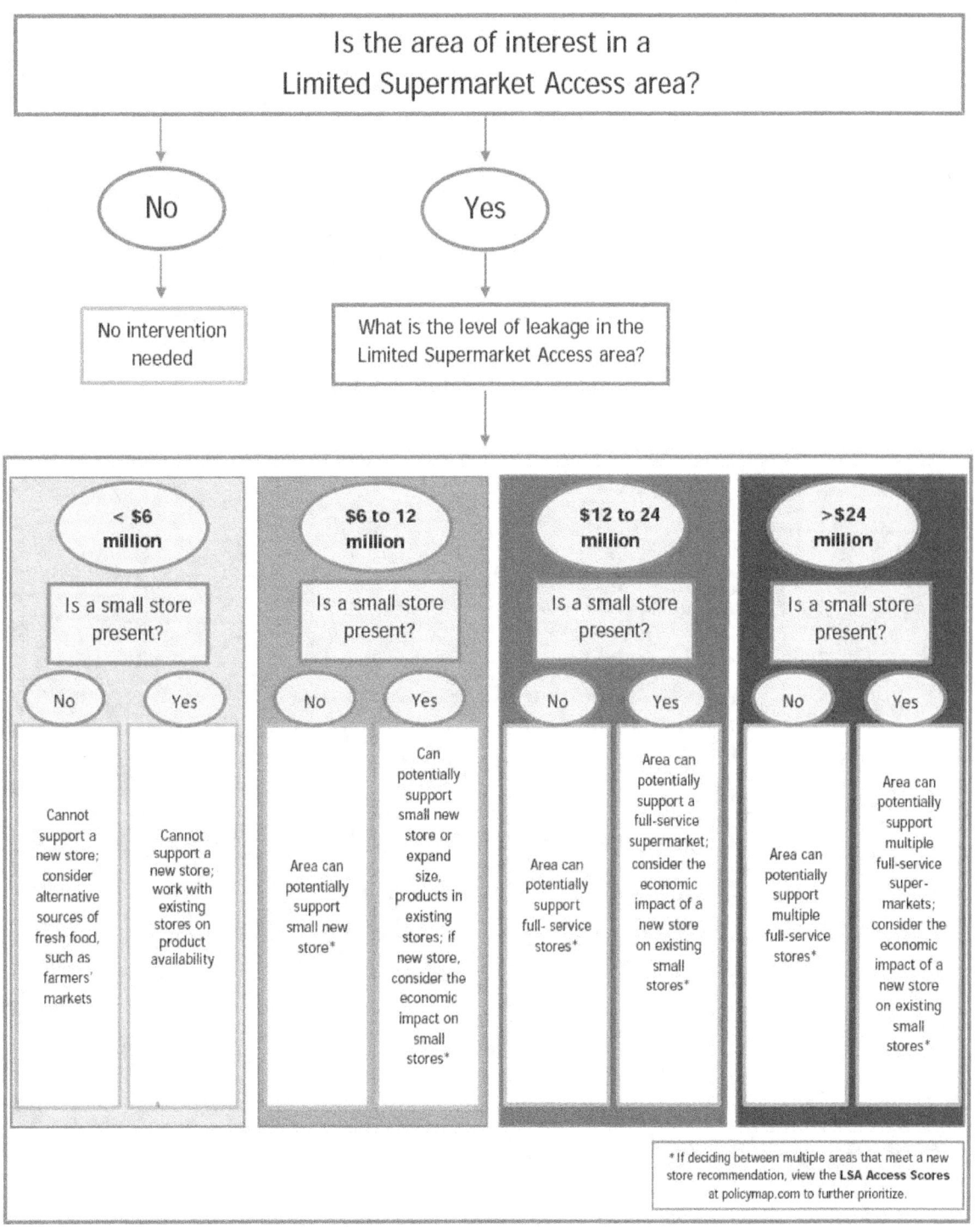

Is the area of interest in a
Limited Supermarket Access area?

No

Yes

No intervention
needed

What is the level of leakage in the
Limited Supermarket Access area?

< $6 million

Is a small store
present?

No — Yes

Cannot support a new store; consider alternative sources of fresh food, such as farmers' markets

Cannot support a new store; work with existing stores on product availability

$6 to 12 million

Is a small store
present?

No — Yes

Area can potentially support small new store*

Can potentially support small new store or expand size, products in existing stores; if new store, consider the economic impact on small stores*

$12 to 24 million

Is a small store
present?

No — Yes

Area can potentially support full-service stores*

Area can potentially support a full-service supermarket; consider the economic impact of a new store on existing small stores*

>$24 million

Is a small store
present?

No — Yes

Area can potentially support multiple full-service stores*

Area can potentially support multiple full-service super-markets; consider the economic impact of a new store on existing small stores*

* If deciding between multiple areas that meet a new store recommendation, view the **LSA Access Scores** at policymap.com to further prioritize.

ENDNOTES

[1] United States Department of Agriculture. "Access to Affordable and Nutritious Food: Measuring and Understanding Food Deserts and Their Consequences." Report to Congress 2009; pp. 1–160.

[2] http://www.cdfifund.gov/what_we_do/resources/Healthy%20Food%20Retail%20Financing%20102411.pdf

[3] Goldstein I., Loethen L., Kako E., Califano C. "CDFI Financing of Supermarkets in Underserved Communities: A Case Study." The Reinvestment Fund, August 2008; pp. 9–14. Available at http://www.trfund.com/resource/downloads/policypubs/TRF_CDFI_SupermarketStudy.pdf.

[4] The Food Marketing Institute (FMI) is a nonprofit association of 1,500 food retailers and wholesalers, their subsidiaries and customers. Food Marketing Institute (FMI), "Access to Healthier Foods: Opportunities and Challenges for Food Retailers in Underserved Areas". July 2011 http://www.fmi.org/docs/health-wellness/Access_To_Healthier_Foods.pdf

[5] 2008 United States Farm Bill, http://www.usda.gov/documents/Bill_6124.pdf.

[6] Walker R., Keane C., Burke J. "Disparities and Access to Healthy Food in the United States: A Review of Food Deserts Literature." *Health & Place* 2010; Vol. 16, No. 5, pp. 876–84.

[7] Beaulac J., Kristjansson E., Cummins S. "A Systematic Review of Food Deserts, 1966–2007." *Preventing Chronic Disease 2009*; Vol. 6, No. 3. http://www.cdc.gov/pcd/issues/2009/jul/08_0163.htm. Accessed 7/29/2010.

[8] Larson N., Story M., Nelson M. "Neighborhood Environments: Disparities in Access to Healthy Foods in the U.S." *American Journal of Preventive Medicine* 2009; Vol. 36, No. 1, pp. 74–81.

[9] Farley T., Rice J., Bodor J. N., Cohen D., Bluthenthal R., Rose D. "Measuring the Food Environment: Shelf Space of Fruits, Vegetables and Snack Foods in Stores." *Journal of Urban Health: Bulletin of the New York Academy of Medicine* 2009; Vol. 86, No. 5, pp. 672–82.

[10] Franco M., Diez Roux A., Glass T., Caballero B., Brancati F. "Neighborhood Characteristics and Availability of Healthy Foods in Baltimore." *American Journal of Preventive Medicine* 2008; Vol. 35, No. 6, pp. 561–67.

[11] The HFAI assesses the availability of eight food groups, assigning points for higher availability of items within each group, to a possible total of 27 points. The eight food groups assessed are nonfat/lowfat milk, fruits, vegetables, lowfat meat, frozen foods, low-sodium foods, 100% whole wheat bread and low-sugar cereals. More information on the HFAI may be found in the "Methods" section of Franco et al, pp. 562–63.

[12] See, for example: Glanz K., Sallis J., Saelens B., Frank L. "Nutrition Environment Measures Survey in Stores (NEMS-S): Development and Evaluation." *American Journal of Preventive Medicine* 2007; Vol. 32, No. 4, pp. 282–89. Also see: Zenk S., Schulz A., Israel B., James S., Bao S., Wilson M. "Fruit and Vegetable Access Differs by Community Racial Composition and Socioeconomic Position in Detroit, Michigan." *Journal of Ethnicity and Disease* 2006; Vol. 16, Winter, pp. 275–80.

[13] For instance, Franco et al. (p. 565) found that "several stores coded as grocery stores in predominantly white, higher-income neighborhoods had a higher availability of healthy foods than did supermarkets in predominantly black neighborhoods."

[14] Short A., Guthman J., Raskin S. "Food Deserts, Oases, or Mirages?: Small Markets and Community Food Security in the San Francisco Bay Area." *Journal of Planning Education and Research* 2007; No. 26, pp. 352–64, especially p. 359.

[15] Hee-Jung S., Gittelsohn J., Kim M., Suratkar S., Sharma S., Anliker J. "A Corner Store Intervention in a Low-Income Urban Community Is Associated with Increased Availability and Sales of Some Healthy Foods." *Public Health Nutrition* 2009; Vol. 12, No. 11, pp. 2060–67.

[16] Kowaleski-Jones L., Fan J. X., Yamada I., Zick C.D., Smith K.R., Brown B. B. (2009). "Alternative Measures of Food Deserts: Fruitful Options or Empty Cupboards?" National Poverty Center Working Paper.

[17] Rose D. , Bodor J. N., Swalm C. M., Rice J. C., Farley T. A., Hutchison P. L. (2009). "Deserts in New Orleans? Illustrations of Urban Food Access and Implications for Policy." National Poverty Center Working Paper.

[18] Go to http://www.ers.usda.gov/Publications/AP/AP036/AP036l.pdf and see Appendix C, p. 131.

[19] http://www.naics.com/CensusCensusfiles/ND445110.HTM

[20] E.g., Apparicio P., Cloutier M., Shearmur R. "The Case of Montréal's Missing Food Deserts: Evaluation of Accessibility to Food

Supermarkets." *International Journal of Health Geographics* 2007; Vol. 6, No. 4. Available at http://www.ij-healthgeographics.com/content/6/1/4. Accessed 7/27/2010.

[21] Kowalski-Jones et al., p. 14.

[22] Sparks A., Bania N., Leete L. "Finding Food Deserts: Methodology and Measurement of Food Access in Portland, Oregon." Paper presented at the joint USDA and National Poverty Center Conference "Understanding the Economic Concepts and Characteristics of Food Access," January 23, 2009. Available at http://www.npc.umich.edu/news/events/food-access/sparks_et_al.pdf. Accessed 7/29/2010, pp. 4–5.

[23] A heat map presents information on both proximity and variety by describing a continuous surface in which "the value of any point on the surface is determined by the number of food outlets within a given search radius (with greater weight given to outlets that are closer to a given point)." Definition found in Neckerman K., Bader M., Purciel M., Yousefzadeh P. "Measuring Food Access in Urban Areas." Paper presented at the joint USDA and National Poverty Center Conference "Understanding the Economic Concepts and Characteristics of Food Access," January 23, 2009. Available at http://www.npc.umich.edu/news/events/food-access/neckerman_et_al.pdf. Accessed 7/29/2010, p. 6.

Heat maps, therefore, are able to depict finer gradations of access, because they are not tied to either pre-designated administrative divisions or a fixed-distance buffer. However, other data, such as detailed demographic information, are often not available at such a detailed level, mitigating the advantages of the heat-map approach.

[24] E.g., Neckerman et al., pp. 9–18.

[25] Kowalski-Jones et al., p. 11; Neckerman et al., p. 20.

[26] Food Desert Locator Documentation (n.d.). *USDA Economic Research Service, Home Page.*
Retrieved August 4, 2011 from http://www.ers.usda.gov/data/foodDesert/documentation.html.

[27] Powell L., Slater S., Mirtcheva D., Bao Y., Chaloupka F. "Food Store Availability and Neighborhood Characteristics in the United States." *Preventive Medicine* 2007; Vol. 44, No. 3, pp. 189–95.

[28] United States Department of Agriculture. "Report to Congress: Access to Affordable and Nutritious Food: Measuring and Understanding Food Deserts and Their Consequences," June 2009. Available at http://www.ers.usda.gov/Publications/AP/AP036/AP036.pdf.

[29] ERS included all full-service supermarkets as defined by TDLinx.

[30] Richardson, K. "Exploring Food Environments: Assessing Access to Nutritious Food." *ArcUser*, Fall 2010. http://www.esri.com/news/arcuser/1010/files/foodataset.pdf

[31] "Evans D. L., Evans W. *The Complete Real Estate Encyclopedia* (New York: McGraw-Hill, 2007).

[32] Strother S., Strother B., Martin B. "Retail Market Estimation for Strategic Economic Development." *Journal of Retail & Leisure Property* 2007; Vol. 8, No. 2, pp. 139–52.

[33] Social Compact. "New Orleans, LA Grocery Gap." http://socialcompact.org/index.php/site/reports/category/reports/

[34] http://www.CensusCensus.gov/econ/

[35] Williams C. "Rethinking the Role of the Retail Sector in Economic Development." *Service Industries Journal* 1997; Vol. 17, No. 2, pp. 205–20.

[36] The CNN Money.com 2009 review of profitability by industry notes that the top 10 most profitable industries in 2008 show profits of 9.9% or greater as percent of revenue; food and drug stores are ranked at 37 and show a 1.5% return. http://money.cnn.com/magazines/fortune/fortune500/2009/performers/industries/profits/

[37] Food Marketing Institute, "Access to Healthier Foods: Opportunities and Challenges for Food Retailers in Underserved Areas." July 2011. Available at http://www.fmi.org/docs/health-wellness/Access_To_Healthier_Foods.pdf.

[38] Standard deviation is a widely used measurement of dispersion. It describes the variability or diversity from the average (mean). A

low standard deviation indicates that the data points tend to be very close to the mean, whereas a high standard deviation indicates that the data is distributed over a large range of values.

[39] TRF opted to use 2000 U. S. census data to calculate car-ownership rates at the block group level, even though more recent data are available from the 2005–2009 American Community Survey (ACS), because ACS data at the block group level has a high margin of error due to the ACS sampling method. While we recognize that the 2000 census is older, TRF's analysis of census and ACS data suggest that car-ownership rates are stable over time. TRF used Public Use Micro Sample (PUMS) data from the 1990 and 2000 decennial censuses and the 2010 ACS to compare changes in car-ownership rates among the 151 cities included in all three data sources. (The city is the smallest available geography in the 2010 ACS and is less prone to having a high margin of error than a census block group or tract.)

The correlation between the 2000 and 2010 values for percent of households with cars among the 151 cities is 0.910 and is statistically significant. Between 1990 and 2000, the correlation coefficient is slightly lower at 0.822 but still statistically significant. While the 151 cities used for this calculation do not represent all cities in the country, they do include a broad range of sizes, from large cities (New York, Los Angeles, Chicago, Philadelphia and Seattle) to mid-sized cities (Grand Rapids, MI; North Las Vegas, NV) and relatively small cities (El Monte, CA; Gary, IN; Norwalk, CA; Hartford, CT; Provo, UT). This persistence in car-ownership rates among a wide range of cities suggests that our use of 2000 data instead of 2010 is unlikely to introduce substantial bias into our results.

The above correlations do not test the stability in more rural areas. However, given the nature of rural development and the tendency for rural households to live much longer distances from the nearest grocery store, car ownership is more essential in rural areas. Thus we expect car-ownership rates to be even more stable in rural areas.

[40] TDLinx is a Nielsen Media company.

[41] For more information on the Trade Dimensions retail site database, see Nielsen's websites at http://ca.nielsen.com/content/nielsen/en_ca/product_families/nielsen_trade_dimensions.html and http://www.plainvanillashell.com/rsdb.asp.

[42] http://www.fmi.org/facts_figs/?fuseaction=superfact

[43] TRF decided to include military commissary stores in the store database. Military commissary stores represent $3,567,408,000 in sales annually (see Appendix I, Table 1), a small total percentage of sales but still a significant amount, and they are a food source for military personnel living on bases; they may also serve military personnel living off base in the surrounding census block groups. While the population of a military base is included in the census count, block groups that are exclusively within a base are not identified. Thus we have no way to measure who does or does not have access and must conclude that shoppers are from the surrounding census block groups. Sales tells us that military personnel are shopping at the commissary stores, so to exclude these stores could result in the false identification of areas as low access, as well as in inaccurate leakage numbers.

[44] Jetter K. M., Cassady D. L. "The Availability and Cost of Healthier Food Alternatives." *American Journal of Preventive Medicine* 2006, pp. 30 and 38–44; Liese A. D., Weis K. E., Pluto D., Smith E., Lawson A. "Food Store Types, Availability and Cost of Foods in a Rural Environment." *Journal of the American Dietetic Association* 2007; No. 107, pp. 1916–23.

[45] Cassady D. C., Jetter K. M., Culp J. (2007). "Is Price a Barrier to Eating More Fruits and Vegetables for Low-Income Families?" *Journal of the American Dietetic Association*: No. 107, pp. 1909–15; Chung C., Myers S. L. "Do the Poor Pay More for Food? An Analysis of Grocery Store Availability and Food Price Disparities." *Journal of Consumer Affairs* 1999; No. 33, pp. 276–96.

[46] TRF's analysis did not include smaller stores and conventional drug stores, although some provide adequate access to food. This decision was based on the difficulty as well as the subjective nature of distinguishing small stores that provide healthy items and the lack of national-level data addressing this question. However, we do recognize that supermarkets are not the only viable source of affordable, nutritious food. We also recognize that not all supermarkets provide high-quality fruits, vegetables, meats and dairy. Accordingly, we describe our methodology as a first step toward identifying areas with concentrations of households with limited access to supermarkets, rather than as the identification of food deserts, which would imply limited access to all healthy food outlets.

[47] FMI Grocer Trends Report, October 2010 http://www.fmi.org/news_releases/index.cfm?fuseaction=mediatext&id=1172.

[48] This calculation excluded military commissary store sales.

[49] Here is one such example citing a USDA and Aldi partnership: http://www.progressivegrocer.com/top-stories/headlines/health-wellness/id33670/aldi-partners-with-usda-for-healthy-eating/.

[50] For example, residents with access to cars might find it easier to shop at supermarkets less frequently but might purchase more food per trip, so that a longer travel time to food might be more acceptable for these residents. One study found these shopping patterns in a case study conducted among low-income residents of Austin, TX. Clifton K. "Mobility Strategies and Food Shopping for Low-Income Families: A Case Study." *Journal of Pianning Education and Research* 2004; No. 23, pp. 402–13.

[51] TRF compared percentages of car ownership from the 2005–2009 ACS data (U.S. Census Bureau) to the 2000 Decennial Census data. Urban block groups showed large differences between datasets. These changes could be caused either by real differences in percentages of car ownership or by methodological differences between the ACS data and the long-form 2000 Census. After spatially mapping out the data and analyzing familiar areas, TRF concluded that the 2000 Census variable of percentage of car ownership more accurately represented on-the-ground car-ownership rates than the 2005–2009 ACS dataset.

[52] Not all combinations of density and car ownership were used to describe neighborhoods. TRF's criteria do not find any extreme low-density, low-car-ownership block groups in the U.S. classification and regression trees (CART). CART analysis was used to identify appropriate density and car-ownership category breakpoints. CART is a *non-parametric decision-tree learning* technique that produces a classification tree of independent variables based on a selected dependent variable that is either categorical or numeric. Distance to nearest store was used as the dependent variable.

[53] NAVTECH (NVT) (owned by Nokia) is a proprietary street center line database. It was used to calculate network distances between block and supermarket locations. NAVTECH is recognized as the leader in providing the highest level of street information in North America for network route calculations and is often included as the base dataset in automobile global positioning systems. This database contains information on road type, one-way streets, turn restrictions, toll roads and road intersections.

[54] The definitions and categories used to identify low-mod tracts and block groups are not universal. To define reference distance, TRF used census income data, specifically local median household income (MHI) as a percent of metro area MHI in 2009. For block groups located outside of census-defined metro areas, the calculation is the local MHI as a percent of state MHI. Variations exist among federal program guidelines on targeted populations. Generally, block groups and tracts with local MHI less than or equal to 30% of area median income (MHI) are considered very low income; low income are those less than or equal to 50% of area median income; moderate income are those less than or equal to 80% of area median income; middle income are those less than or equal to 120% of area median income; and block groups and tracts above 120% are considered the upper-income areas.

[55] For more information on LISA analysis, see Anselin, L. "Local Indicators of Spatial Association–LISA." *Geographical Analysis* 1995; Vol. 27, No. 2, 93–115.

[56] Percentage of income spent on "food at home" for each household-income category is obtained from the 2009 Consumer Expenditure Survey, a quarterly survey conducted by the Bureau of Labor Statistics of the U.S. Department of Labor that provides information on American buying habits.

[57] Low-income block groups are those with median household incomes at or below 80% of their respective area median; a block group's area median is either the metropolitan-area's household median or the median of its state's non metropolitan households.

[58] As was previously mentioned, if a financing program's mission is more focused on improving access in low-income areas, perhaps a weighted composite score would be more appropriate. One could apply a 25% weight to the percentage of population in LSAs and a 75% weight to the percentage of LSA population in low-income areas.

[59] http://www.census.gov/population/metro/about/index.html

[60] Evans D. L., Evans W.; http://financial-dictionary.thefreedictionary.com/leakage.

Appendix 1:
Store Categorizations and Descriptions as Defined by Trade Dimensions

Supermarket, Conventional: A supermarket is a full-line, self-service grocery store with an annual sales volume of $2 million or more. This definition applies to individual stores regardless of total company size or sales and therefore includes both chain and independent locations. Examples: Kroger, Food Lion, IGA, Cub Foods

Supercenter: A supercenter is a retail unit that combines a full-line supermarket and a full-line discount merchandiser under one roof. It may have separate or combined checkouts. Examples: Wal-Mart Supercenter, Meijer Supermarket

Supermarket, Limited Assortment: A limited-assortment supermarket has a limited selection of items in a reduced number of categories. These stores typically offer low pricing. It differs from a conventional supermarket principally in the reduced size and depth of produce and nonfood categories such as health and beauty care (HBC), cleaning supplies, paper products and general merchandise. A limited-assortment supermarket has few if any service departments and less product variety than a conventional supermarket. Examples: Aldi Food Store, Save-A-Lot

Natural/Gourmet Foods: A natural or gourmet foods supermarket is a self-service grocery store primarily offering natural, organic or gourmet foods. These stores will focus product offerings around either fresh produce and natural products or gourmet foods such as upscale oils, spices, cheese, meats and produce. Natural/gourmet foods supermarkets typically have expanded fresh food departments and/or prepared food selections. These supermarkets also typically have a limited selection, if any, of HBC and general merchandise. A natural/gourmet foods supermarket does not have over 50% of its product offerings in one category, as is the case with traditional butcher shops, delis, produce stands or nutritional-supplement stores. Note: Ethnic supermarkets are not considered natural/gourmet foods supermarkets. Examples: Trader Joe's, Whole Foods, Dean & DeLuca

Warehouse Grocery: This is a grocery store with limited service that eliminates frills and concentrates on price appeal. Items are displayed for sale in their original shipping cartons rather than being placed individually on shelves. This type of store also sells bulk food and large-size items. Examples: Cash & Carry, Smart & Final

Conventional/Wholesale Club: The Wholesale Club Trade Channel includes membership club stores that distribute packaged and bulk foods and general merchandise. They are characterized by high volume on a restricted line of popular merchandise in a no-frills environment. The average club stocks approximately 4,000 SKUs, 40% of which are grocery items. Examples: BJ's, Sam's Club

Military Commissary: This is a grocery store operated by the U.S. Defense Commissary Agency within the confines of a military installation. A commissary can fit within any of the grocery formats. Examples: Fort Hood DECA Commissary, Fort Riley DECA Commissary

Superette/Small Grocery: A superette is a grocery store with a sales volume ranging from $1 to $2 million annually. Typically, superettes are independent, but many are affiliated with groups such as IGA, Inc. A "small grocery" is defined as a grocery store with sales below $1 million annually. These are also known as Mom & Pop stores. Examples: Country Market, Superior Markets

Appendix 2: Leakage Diagram

The diagram below shows the methods used to calculate and allocate sales to a sample of block groups.

Step I. Calculate distance to store for each block with a positive low access score.

Step II. Identify total sales from each limited service store within those blocks' reference distance.

Step III. Allocate a percentage of sales to each block based on its share of the total population in all blocks served by limited service store(s).

Step IV. Aggregate total sales for each block to the census block group.

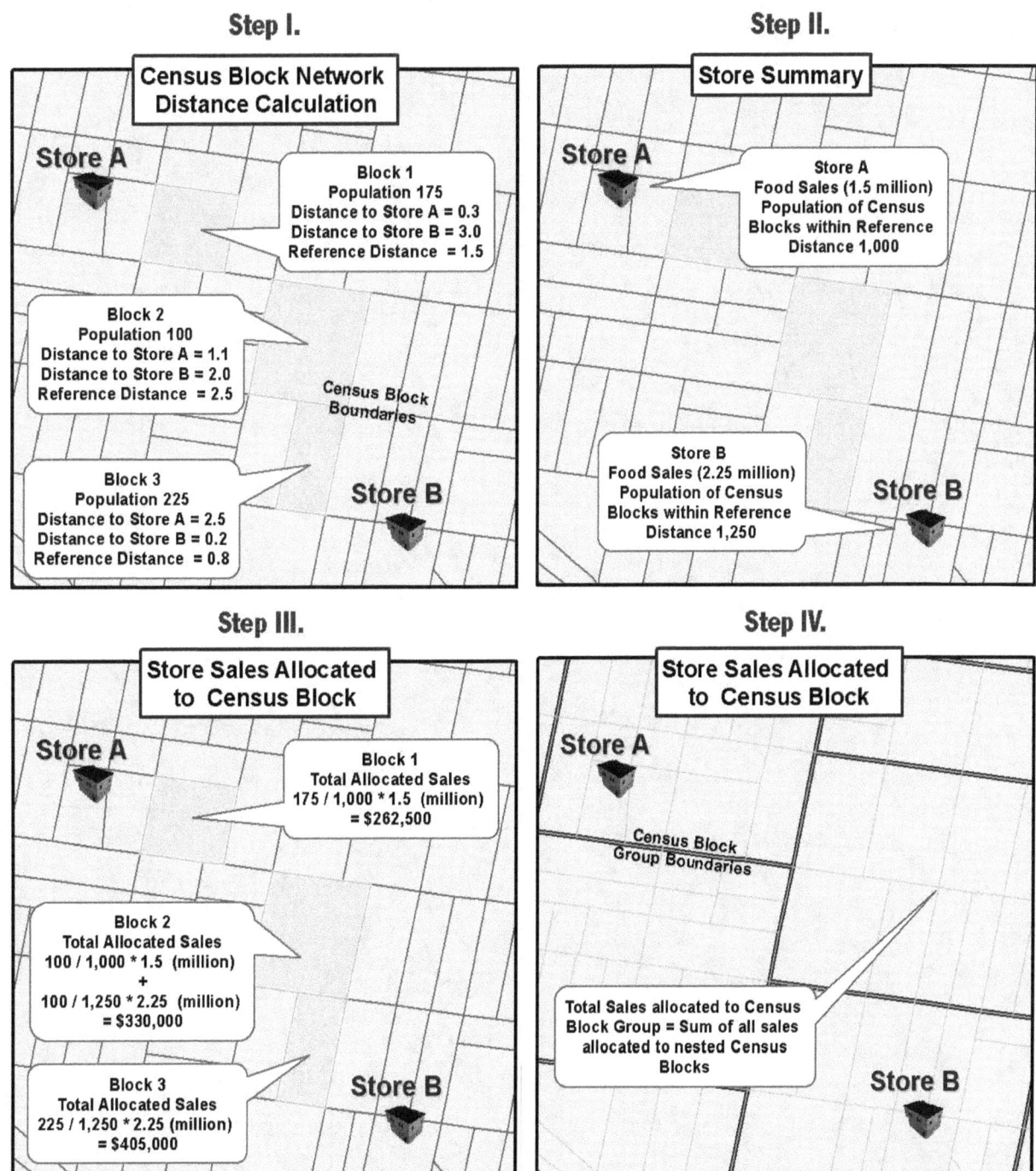

Appendix 3:
Detailed LSA Results by Geography

This appendix uses two variables to rank selected geographies:

- *Percentage of total population living in LSAs*: Measures the relative size of a place's LSA problem regardless of income status. This variable is referred to as the "relative size" of the LSA problem.

- *Percentage of LSA population living in low-income block groups*: Measures the extent to which the LSA problem is located in low-income areas. Areas ranking high on this measure do not necessarily have the largest percentage of population in LSA areas, but the LSA burden is felt more strongly in low-income areas. This variable is referred to as the low-income burden of the LSA problem.[1]

In addition to showing the values for these two variables, the tables presented below show each variable's rank and a composite rank for each geographic category, defined as follows:

Rank for percentage of total population in LSA: Indicates the relative size of each place's LSA problem compared to its peer geographies. The percentages of total population living in LSAs are ranked in descending order, with the largest value ranked first.

Rank for percentage of LSA population living in low-income block groups: Indicates the size of the low-income burden of the LSA problem within each geography compared to its peer geographies by ranking the percentage of LSA population living in low-income block groups in descending order, with the largest value ranked first.

Composite rank: Represents each geography's average of the two rankings defined above, resulting in a combined measure of each place's relative size and the low-income burden of its LSA problem compared to those of peer geographies. [2]

The tables in this appendix list states, Core Based Statistical Areas (CBSAs) and U.S. census places (such as cities and towns) in ascending order by the composite rank for the aforementioned variables. For example, Table A-1 shows that Louisiana ranks fifth in its percentage of population living in LSAs (15%) and 18th in its percentage of LSA population living in low-income block groups (49%), resulting in a composite score of 11.5 (the average of 5 and 18). This ranks fourth among state composite scores. When areas have tying composite scores, the area with the larger population living in LSAs is given the higher composite rank. This process is applied to all other geographies listed below, with CBSAs and census places grouped into subcategories based on their total populations to account for values ranging from less than 10,000 to several million.

---

[1] Low-income block groups are those with median household incomes at or below 80% of their respective area median; a block group's area median is either the metropolitan area household median or the median of its state's nonmetropolitan households.

[2] When areas have tying composite scores, the area with the larger population in LSAs is given the higher composite rank.

States

Table A-1 lists states and the District of Columbia in order of their composite ranking. The average state has 8.6% of its population living in LSAs, 42% of which lives in low-income areas. The District of Columbia ranks first in both measures, showing dramatically higher percentages than all states: 24% for relative size and 91% for low-income burden. With the exception of Pennsylvania and Rhode Island, the remaining top 10 states tend to rank significantly higher in one variable than the other. Louisiana and West Virginia rank high in relative size of the problem, yet they rank near the middle in low-income burden. Connecticut, Illinois, Ohio and Tennessee exhibit the opposite scenario, while New York shows relatively similar rankings for both variables (19th and 14th). Figure A-1 shows a scatter plot for relative demand (X axis) and low-income burden (Y axis) for all states listed in Table A-1. The two variables are not significantly correlated.

Table A-1: LSA Figures by State

Geography	Total Population	Total LSA Population	Total % of Pop in LSA	Rank for Total % of Pop in LSA	% of LSA Pop in Low-Income Area	Rank for % of LSA Pop in Low-Income Area	Composite Rank
Pennsylvania	12,698,826	1,528,284	12%	7	54%	4	1
Rhode Island	1,052,729	148,745	14%	6	53%	9	2
Louisiana	4,532,703	694,257	15%	4	49%	17	3
Connecticut	3,572,522	273,595	8%	22	62%	1	4
Illinois	12,827,020	1,048,199	8%	19	53%	6	5
Ohio	11,534,079	939,126	8%	20	54%	5	6
West Virginia	1,852,161	309,237	17%	2	46%	24	7
Tennessee	6,344,653	449,129	7%	25	59%	3	8
New York	19,375,996	1,459,034	8%	18	51%	13	9
Maryland	5,773,198	602,845	10%	12	48%	19	10
Wisconsin	5,685,495	402,420	7%	27	53%	7	11
Massachusetts	6,545,161	777,880	12%	9	42%	27	12
Texas	25,141,913	3,427,416	14%	5	39%	32	13
Michigan	9,883,320	836,227	8%	21	49%	16	14
New Jersey	8,789,199	1,024,563	12%	8	40%	29	15
Missouri	5,987,588	389,210	7%	26	52%	11	16
Florida	18,798,030	1,313,487	7%	24	49%	15	17
Arizona	6,390,253	717,791	11%	10	40%	30	18
New Mexico	2,058,796	373,003	18%	1	30%	39	19
Georgia	9,686,326	569,700	6%	31	52%	10	20
Kansas	2,852,631	175,043	6%	36	53%	8	21
Mississippi	2,966,599	156,599	5%	43	60%	2	22
Delaware	897,753	102,009	11%	11	37%	34	23
Virginia	7,999,101	451,048	6%	32	51%	14	24
North Dakota	672,520	111,080	17%	3	21%	44	25
Minnesota	5,302,669	483,458	9%	16	39%	33	26
Kentucky	4,338,867	302,343	7%	28	47%	21	27
Oklahoma	3,750,450	375,630	10%	13	33%	36	28
Wyoming	563,453	43,178	8%	23	42%	28	29
Nevada	2,700,317	272,161	10%	14	30%	38	30
South Carolina	4,624,218	263,033	6%	35	47%	20	31
California	37,244,395	1,680,131	5%	38	48%	18	32
Indiana	6,481,763	391,779	6%	34	46%	22	33
Montana	989,100	102,095	10%	15	27%	42	34
Arkansas	2,915,160	73,957	3%	46	52%	12	35
South Dakota	814,114	73,127	9%	17	13%	46	36
Alabama	4,778,501	221,031	5%	41	46%	23	37
North Carolina	9,533,763	473,802	5%	39	42%	26	38
Colorado	5,028,054	258,174	5%	40	43%	25	39
New Hampshire	1,315,982	88,897	7%	30	35%	35	40
Utah	2,763,220	200,993	7%	29	28%	40	41
Iowa	3,045,618	160,181	5%	42	40%	31	42
Washington	6,722,563	420,135	6%	33	20%	45	43
Nebraska	1,824,456	102,008	6%	37	28%	41	44
Oregon	3,829,991	99,673	3%	45	31%	37	45
Maine	1,328,022	71,968	5%	44	24%	43	46
Idaho	1,567,197	39,085	2%	47	10%	47	47
Vermont	625,574	12,591	2%	48	0%	48	48

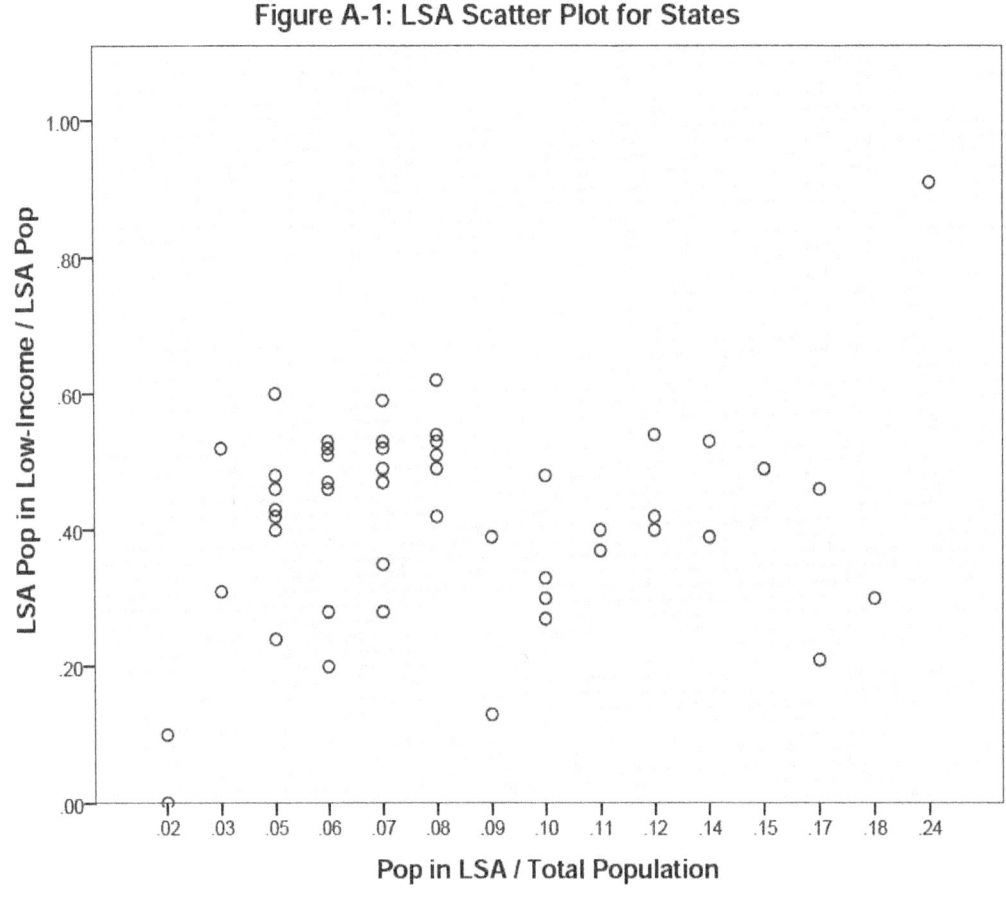

Figure A-1: LSA Scatter Plot for States

Core Based Statistical Areas (metropolitan and micropolitan areas)

Major Metropolitan Areas (Populations Greater Than 1 Million)

The average major metropolitan area has 9% of its population living in LSAs, 52% of which lives in low-income areas. Table A-2.1 ranks metro areas with more than one million residents. The Memphis area ranks first overall, with the low-income burden being the primary driver (fifth rank at 75%). The Pittsburgh and Richmond metro areas serve as a perfect example of how prioritization is particular to a program's mission: the relative size of Pittsburgh's LSA problem is nearly twice that of Richmond's (18% vs. 10%; fifth rank vs. 20th); however, Richmond's low-income burden is dramatically higher than Pittsburgh's (84% vs. 57%; third rank vs. 18th), resulting in identical composite rankings.[3] Notice that San Antonio ranks first in relative size of LSA problem, yet the problem relative to other large cities is not unique to low-income areas, as the city's low-income burden ranks 44th.

Metropolitan Areas with Populations of 500,000 to 1 Million

The average metropolitan area with a population between 500,000 and 1 million has 9.5% of its population living in LSAs, 49% of which lives in low-income areas. Table A-2.2 ranks metro areas with populations between 500,000 and 1 million, with the Albany area ranked first, followed by Baton Rouge, New Haven, Harrisburg, and Wichita in the top five. The McAllen-Edinburg-Mission metro area has the highest rank for the relative size of its LSA problem but ranks 31st in low-income burden, resulting in 9th overall. Des Moines exhibits the opposite features, being ranked first in low-income burden, 33rd in the problem's relative size and 11th overall. Even though Des Moines does not show an overwhelming percentage of its population in LSAs, the concentration of that population in low-income areas is remarkably high (90%).

Metropolitan Areas with Populations of 250,000 to 500,000

The average metropolitan area with a population between 250,000 and 500,000 has 8.9% of its population living in LSAs, 47% of which lives in low-income areas. Table A-2.3 ranks metro areas with population between 250,000 and 500,000, with the Trenton, NJ area ranked first, followed by Columbus, GA; Savannah, GA; Erie, PA and Atlantic City, NJ in the top five. The Shreveport, LA area ranks at the top for relative size of the problem but ranks 45th in low-income burden, resulting in an overall ranking of 14th. Kingsport-Bristol, TN exhibits the opposite, being ranked first in low-income burden, 59th in the problem's relative size and 11th overall. Though Kingsport does not show an overwhelming percentage of its population in LSAs, the concentration of that population in low-income areas is remarkably high (100%).

Metropolitan Areas with Populations of Less Than 250,000

The average metropolitan area with a population of less than 250,000 has 9.6% of its population living in LSAs, 38% of which lives in low-income areas. Table A-2.4 ranks metropolitan areas with populations of less than 250,000, with the Decatur, IL metro area ranked first, followed by Muskegon-Norton Shores, MI; College Station-Bryan, TX; Lafayette, IN and Show Low, AZ in the top five. The Lawton, OK metro area ranks first in relative size but ranks 81st in low-income burden, dropping it to 28th overall. Topeka, KS exhibits the opposite, being ranked first in low-income burden and 84th in relative size, for 34th overall.

---

[3] As was previously mentioned, if a financing program's mission is more focused on improving access in low-income areas, perhaps a weighted composite score would be more appropriate: one could apply a 25% weight to the percentage of population in LSAs and a 75% weight to the percentage of LSA population in low-income areas.

Micropolitan Areas

The average micropolitan area has 13% of its population living in LSAs, 24% of which lives in low-income areas. Table A-2.5 ranks all 257 micropolitan areas without stratification by population. Micropolitan statistical areas must have at least one urban cluster of at least 10,000 residents but no more than 50,000, and they tend to be much smaller than metropolitan areas. For all micropolitan areas with at least one LSA, population ranges in size from just over 12,000 (Tallulah, LA) to roughly 190,000 (Torrington, CT), averaging 59,324.

Amsterdam, NY has the highest composite ranking among all micropolitan areas, followed by Macomb, IL; Clarksdale, MS; Tallulah, LA and Gallup, NM in the top five. Rio Grande, TX has the top ranking for relative size but ranks 117th in low-income burden, dropping it to 25th overall. Numerous micropolitan areas exhibit the opposite, with 100% values for

Table A-2.1: LSA Figures for Major Metro Areas with Populations Greater Than 1,000,000

Geography	Total Population	Total LSA Population	Total % of Pop in LSA	Rank for Total % of Pop in LSA	% of LSA Pop in Low-Income Area	Rank for % of LSA Pop in Low-Income Area	Composite Rank
Memphis, TN-MS-AR	1,315,850	155,419	12%	14	75%	5	1
Pittsburgh, PA	2,355,231	422,513	18%	5	57%	18	2
Richmond, VA	1,257,997	124,662	10%	20	84%	3	3
New Orleans-Metairie-Kenner, LA	1,167,694	242,172	21%	3	56%	20	4
Philadelphia-Camden-Wilmington, PA-NJ-DE-MD	5,964,299	796,746	13%	8	57%	17	5
Milwaukee-Waukesha-West Allis, WI	1,555,512	167,167	11%	17	71%	8	6
St. Louis, MO-IL	2,836,702	383,039	14%	6	50%	25	7
Baltimore-Towson, MD	2,710,302	350,267	13%	10	55%	22	8
Cleveland-Elyria-Mentor, OH	2,076,526	206,908	10%	19	61%	15	9
Buffalo-Niagara Falls, NY	1,135,409	210,555	19%	4	46%	33	10
Rochester, NY	1,054,223	142,498	14%	7	48%	31	11
Cincinnati-Middletown, OH-KY-IN	2,129,957	287,398	13%	11	49%	28	12
Providence-New Bedford-Fall River, RI-MA	1,600,594	192,940	12%	13	50%	26	13
Tampa-St. Petersburg-Clearwater, FL	2,782,537	194,775	7%	29	64%	11	14
Chicago-Naperville-Joliet, IL-IN-WI	9,458,230	765,637	8%	23	56%	19	15
Kansas City, MO-KS	2,035,230	73,929	4%	42	87%	2	16
Miami-Fort Lauderdale-Miami Beach, FL	5,563,854	471,392	8%	24	55%	21	17
San Antonio, TX	2,141,925	504,912	24%	1	35%	44	18
Washington-Arlington-Alexandria, DC-VA-MD-WV	5,581,672	326,925	6%	33	62%	14	19
Detroit-Warren-Livonia, MI	4,296,154	437,681	10%	18	48%	30	20
Houston-Baytown-Sugar Land, TX	5,945,811	753,656	13%	9	39%	40	21
Jacksonville, FL	1,345,526	58,822	4%	45	75%	4	22
Dallas-Fort Worth-Arlington, TX	6,371,469	722,864	11%	15	44%	35	23
Minneapolis-St. Paul-Bloomington, MN-WI	3,279,239	383,762	12%	12	40%	38	24
Columbus, OH	1,836,118	141,760	8%	27	54%	23	25
Austin-Round Rock, TX	1,716,227	400,195	23%	2	28%	48	26
Virginia Beach-Norfolk-Newport News, VA-NC	1,671,213	106,962	6%	37	63%	13	27
Raleigh-Cary, NC	1,130,501	25,155	2%	49	92%	1	28
Birmingham-Hoover, AL	1,127,897	109,552	10%	21	49%	29	29
Los Angeles-Long Beach-Santa Ana, CA	12,825,385	450,523	4%	41	67%	10	30
Nashville-Davidson--Murfreesboro, TN	1,589,709	70,446	4%	44	71%	7	31
Boston-Cambridge-Quincy, MA-NH	4,550,897	496,617	11%	16	42%	36	32
Hartford-West Hartford-East Hartford, CT	1,211,964	51,401	4%	46	74%	6	33
Louisville, KY-IN	1,283,234	81,679	6%	38	59%	16	34
Charlotte-Gastonia-Concord, NC-SC	1,757,665	74,306	4%	43	64%	12	35
Salt Lake City, UT	1,123,900	27,604	2%	50	68%	9	36
Atlanta-Sandy Springs-Marietta, GA	5,268,182	356,313	7%	28	47%	32	37
San Francisco-Oakland-Fremont, CA	4,333,418	209,260	5%	39	51%	24	38
Phoenix-Mesa-Scottsdale, AZ	4,191,789	325,011	8%	26	41%	37	39
New York-Northern New Jersey-Long Island, NY-NJ-PA	18,894,316	1,190,504	6%	32	44%	34	40
Orlando, FL	2,134,116	111,459	5%	40	49%	27	41
Riverside-San Bernardino-Ontario, CA	4,224,123	346,421	8%	25	37%	43	42
Oklahoma City, OK	1,252,690	115,170	9%	22	30%	46	43
Indianapolis, IN	1,756,113	119,733	7%	31	39%	41	44
Sacramento--Arden-Arcade--Roseville, CA	2,148,007	133,443	6%	36	40%	39	45
Las Vegas-Paradise, NV	1,951,178	128,981	7%	30	31%	45	46
Denver-Aurora, CO	2,519,310	159,236	6%	35	38%	42	47
Seattle-Tacoma-Bellevue, WA	3,438,719	193,158	6%	34	23%	50	48
Portland-Vancouver-Beaverton, OR-WA	2,225,457	47,821	2%	48	29%	47	49
San Diego-Carlsbad-San Marcos, CA	3,095,171	108,149	3%	47	24%	49	50
San Jose-Sunnyvale-Santa Clara, CA	1,836,506	23,147	1%	51	9%	51	51

Table A-2.2: LSA Figures for Metro Areas with Populations Between 500,000 and 1,000,000

Geography	Total Population	Total LSA Population	Total % of Pop in LSA	Rank for Total % of Pop in LSA	% of LSA Pop in Low-Income Area	Rank for % of LSA Pop in Low-Income Area	Composite Rank
Albany-Schenectady-Troy, NY	870,462	134,880	15%	7	65%	9	1
Baton Rouge, LA	802,302	86,095	11%	15	77%	3	2
New Haven-Milford, CT	862,229	115,382	13%	11	67%	8	3
Harrisburg-Carlisle, PA	549,353	96,668	18%	4	58%	18	4
Wichita, KS	623,024	60,649	10%	20	75%	4	5
Springfield, MA	692,755	112,803	16%	6	56%	21	6
Youngstown-Warren-Boardman, OH-PA	565,509	67,411	12%	14	58%	17	7
El Paso, TX	800,634	95,763	12%	13	57%	19	8
McAllen-Edinburg-Mission, TX	774,636	320,982	41%	1	45%	31	9
Greensboro-High Point, NC	723,683	48,113	7%	26	71%	6	10
Des Moines, IA	569,534	33,474	6%	33	90%	1	11
Bakersfield, CA	839,430	50,302	6%	31	71%	5	12
Poughkeepsie-Newburgh-Middletown, NY	670,117	135,557	20%	3	44%	33	13
Chattanooga, TN-GA	528,050	32,481	6%	35	81%	2	14
Tulsa, OK	937,378	67,275	7%	25	62%	14	15
Fresno, CA	930,636	77,872	8%	23	59%	16	16
Charleston-North Charleston, SC	664,439	72,613	11%	17	54%	23	17
Tucson, AZ	979,978	202,777	21%	2	31%	40	18
Knoxville, TN	697,848	77,756	11%	16	50%	26	19
Dayton, OH	841,255	47,848	6%	30	63%	13	20
Akron, OH	703,276	67,303	10%	19	52%	24	21
Syracuse, NY	662,343	75,392	11%	18	51%	25	22
Scranton--Wilkes-Barre, PA	563,331	41,179	7%	29	61%	15	23
Jackson, MS	538,923	33,368	6%	34	65%	11	24
Worcester, MA	798,228	110,950	14%	9	32%	38	25
Allentown-Bethlehem-Easton, PA-NJ	821,031	101,271	12%	12	40%	36	26
Albuquerque, NM	886,993	147,171	17%	5	16%	44	27
Bradenton-Sarasota-Venice, FL	702,196	49,287	7%	27	54%	22	28
Ogden-Clearfield, UT	547,057	29,412	5%	40	65%	10	29
Little Rock-North Little Rock, AR	699,723	19,360	3%	44	71%	7	30
Greenville, SC	636,825	52,896	8%	24	50%	27	31
Toledo, OH	651,380	55,889	9%	22	46%	30	32
Stockton, CA	685,071	25,280	4%	42	64%	12	33
Bridgeport-Stamford-Norwalk, CT	916,108	48,827	5%	36	56%	20	34
Palm Bay-Melbourne-Titusville, FL	543,278	74,660	14%	10	11%	46	35
Provo-Orem, UT	526,678	77,075	15%	8	5%	48	36
Colorado Springs, CO	645,447	44,250	7%	28	45%	32	37
Durham, NC	504,276	49,377	10%	21	30%	41	38
Columbia, SC	767,471	35,783	5%	37	46%	29	39
Madison, WI	568,422	29,326	5%	39	48%	28	40
Cape Coral-Fort Myers, FL	618,573	37,562	6%	32	26%	42	41
Omaha-Council Bluffs, NE-IA	865,324	34,307	4%	41	42%	35	42
Lakeland, FL	601,963	31,202	5%	38	23%	43	43
Augusta-Richmond County, GA-SC	556,733	12,258	2%	47	43%	34	44
Grand Rapids-Wyoming, MI	774,136	23,557	3%	43	32%	39	45
Lancaster, PA	519,370	17,220	3%	45	36%	37	46
Boise City-Nampa, ID	616,434	8,347	1%	48	16%	45	47
Portland-South Portland-Biddeford, ME	514,035	13,368	3%	46	8%	47	48

Table A-2.3: LSA Figures for Metro Areas with Populations Between 250,000 and 500,000

Geography	Total Population	Total LSA Population	Total % of Pop in LSA	Rank for Total % of Pop in LSA	% of LSA Pop in Low-Income Area	Rank for % of LSA Pop in Low-Income Area	Composite Rank
Trenton-Ewing, NJ	366,608	62,535	17%	11	70%	17	1
Columbus, GA-AL	294,919	36,997	13%	17	73%	11	2
Savannah, GA	347,596	38,272	11%	22	83%	7	3
Erie, PA	280,523	34,465	12%	20	71%	13	4
Atlantic City, NJ	274,537	58,108	21%	4	57%	30	5
Lexington-Fayette, KY	472,040	53,010	11%	21	70%	15	6
Lansing-East Lansing, MI	464,028	64,196	14%	15	62%	22	7
Fort Wayne, IN	416,160	28,244	7%	34	94%	5	8
Hagerstown-Martinsburg, MD-WV	269,092	39,557	15%	14	59%	25	9
Ann Arbor, MI	344,783	65,925	19%	6	53%	34	10
Corpus Christi, TX	428,043	96,968	23%	2	43%	40	11
Beaumont-Port Arthur, TX	388,667	33,613	9%	30	71%	12	12
Kalamazoo-Portage, MI	326,584	37,560	12%	19	59%	24	13
Shreveport-Bossier City, LA	398,559	108,994	27%	1	37%	45	14
Rockford, IL	349,313	24,461	7%	36	76%	10	15
Reno-Sparks, NV	425,375	81,074	19%	5	38%	43	16
Roanoke, VA	308,701	52,525	17%	12	49%	36	17
Ocala, FL	331,247	38,000	11%	23	57%	27	18
Binghamton, NY	251,607	42,940	17%	13	49%	37	19
Manchester-Nashua, NH	400,375	71,833	18%	7	38%	44	20
York-Hanover, PA	434,800	72,230	17%	10	38%	42	21
Brownsville-Harlingen, TX	406,129	89,288	22%	3	35%	49	22
Norwich-New London, CT	273,969	34,308	13%	18	51%	35	23
Lafayette, LA	273,846	18,600	7%	39	71%	14	24
South Bend-Mishawaka, IN-MI	319,213	33,033	10%	26	56%	31	25
Utica-Rome, NY	299,301	32,102	11%	24	55%	33	26
Mobile, AL	412,889	29,524	7%	35	59%	23	27
Charleston, WV	304,158	53,386	18%	8	34%	50	28
Visalia-Porterville, CA	442,011	17,624	4%	52	82%	8	29
Vallejo-Fairfield, CA	413,767	23,136	6%	42	69%	18	30
Deltona-Daytona Beach-Ormond Beach, FL	494,502	25,421	5%	44	68%	19	31
Kingsport-Bristol-Bristol, TN-VA	309,474	10,090	3%	59	100%	4	32
Canton-Massillon, OH	404,283	8,070	2%	62	100%	2	33
Duluth, MN-WI	279,666	49,520	18%	9	27%	55	34
Winston-Salem, NC	477,702	36,157	8%	33	55%	32	35
Flint, MI	425,782	21,209	5%	45	68%	20	36
Peoria, IL	379,054	51,667	14%	16	32%	51	37
Eugene-Springfield, OR	351,601	5,306	2%	64	100%	3	38
Huntington-Ashland, WV-KY-OH	287,596	18,703	7%	38	57%	29	39
Spokane, WA	471,082	6,849	1%	70	100%	1	40
Lubbock, TX	284,815	30,348	11%	25	37%	46	41
Pensacola-Ferry Pass-Brent, FL	448,904	18,148	4%	51	64%	21	42
Santa Barbara-Santa Maria, CA	423,763	20,313	5%	46	57%	26	43
Wilmington, NC	362,246	8,416	2%	63	76%	9	44
Fort Smith, AR-OK	298,484	6,601	2%	66	90%	6	45
Huntsville, AL	417,502	12,649	3%	57	70%	16	46
Lynchburg, VA	252,541	26,246	10%	27	37%	47	47
Green Bay, WI	306,195	22,913	7%	37	45%	39	48
Port St. Lucie, FL	423,968	23,743	6%	41	46%	38	49
Davenport-Moline-Rock Island, IA-IL	379,538	33,742	9%	31	27%	54	50
Killeen-Temple-Fort Hood, TX	405,215	37,001	9%	29	16%	59	51
Bremerton-Silverdale, WA	251,090	16,641	7%	40	37%	48	52
Montgomery, AL	374,432	35,501	9%	32	21%	58	53
Naples-Marco Island, FL	321,460	5,528	2%	65	57%	28	54
Clarksville, TN-KY	273,920	10,937	4%	55	39%	41	55
Olympia, WA	252,136	25,198	10%	28	0%	71	56
Asheville, NC	424,737	17,081	4%	53	27%	53	57
Fayetteville, NC	366,305	15,504	4%	54	29%	52	58
Merced, CA	255,311	13,711	5%	50	26%	56	59
Salinas, CA	414,998	19,057	5%	47	0%	63	60
Evansville, IN-KY	358,571	17,256	5%	48	0%	64	61
Cedar Rapids, IA	257,904	16,118	6%	43	0%	70	62
Spartanburg, SC	284,121	12,830	5%	49	0%	66	63
Hickory-Lenoir-Morganton, NC	365,390	10,343	3%	58	10%	62	64
Reading, PA	411,336	6,645	2%	61	12%	60	65
Holland-Grand Haven, MI	263,797	10,066	4%	56	0%	68	66
Santa Rosa-Petaluma, CA	483,749	5,645	1%	69	23%	57	67
San Luis Obispo-Paso Robles, CA	269,545	8,992	3%	60	0%	67	68
Gainesville, FL	264,360	4,318	2%	67	11%	61	69
Boulder, CO	318,080	869	0%	71	0%	65	70
Santa Cruz-Watsonville, CA	262,265	5,704	2%	68	0%	69	71

Table A-2.4: LSA Figures for Metro Areas with Populations Less Than 250,000

Geography	Total Population	Total LSA Population	Total % of Pop in LSA	Rank for Total % of Pop in LSA	% of LSA Pop in Low-Income Area	Rank for % of LSA Pop in Low-Income Area	Composite Rank
Decatur, IL	110,726	20,260	18%	15	81%	16	1
Muskegon-Norton Shores, MI	172,186	25,131	15%	29	85%	12	2
College Station-Bryan, TX	228,644	39,183	17%	17	61%	29	3
Lafayette, IN	201,731	31,146	15%	26	66%	24	4
Show Low, AZ	107,417	17,427	16%	24	63%	26	5
Racine, WI	195,337	31,253	16%	21	61%	30	6
Monroe, LA	176,384	45,279	26%	5	50%	46	7
Houma-Bayou Cane-Thibodaux, LA	208,158	57,119	27%	2	48%	52	8
Pueblo, CO	159,001	30,311	19%	11	51%	45	9
Sioux City, IA-NE-SD	143,521	29,835	21%	9	50%	47	10
Janesville, WI	160,296	24,529	15%	30	62%	27	11
Cheyenne, WY	91,712	14,050	15%	32	65%	25	12
Amarillo, TX	249,818	33,584	13%	35	66%	23	13
Bloomington-Normal, IL	169,507	27,083	16%	22	54%	36	14
Lewiston-Auburn, ME	107,652	13,569	13%	41	76%	18	15
Altoona, PA	127,041	21,981	17%	19	53%	41	16
Farmington, NM	130,017	35,587	27%	4	45%	59	17
Casper, WY	75,431	9,175	12%	49	76%	19	18
Athens-Clarke County, GA	192,538	16,155	8%	66	100%	3	19
Santa Fe, NM	144,136	30,794	21%	8	42%	62	20
Kingston, NY	182,430	36,578	20%	10	41%	63	21
Wheeling, WV-OH	147,860	28,711	19%	12	42%	61	22
Kankakee-Bradley, IL	113,432	10,975	10%	59	85%	14	23
Gulfport-Biloxi, MS	248,763	24,437	10%	55	69%	22	24
Saginaw-Saginaw Township North, MI	200,169	15,964	8%	63	83%	15	25
Niles-Benton Harbor, MI	156,813	15,558	10%	58	75%	20	26
Alexandria, LA	153,885	41,292	27%	3	26%	79	27
Lawton, OK	124,062	51,462	41%	1	23%	81	28
Macon, GA	232,278	15,279	7%	74	91%	9	29
El Centro, CA	174,488	25,752	15%	28	46%	56	30
Yuba City, CA	166,849	42,703	26%	6	27%	78	31
Brunswick, GA	112,364	8,444	8%	73	88%	11	32
Waco, TX	234,904	39,561	17%	16	35%	69	33
Topeka, KS	233,805	11,186	5%	84	100%	1	34
Springfield, IL	210,090	27,034	13%	37	49%	49	35
Morgantown, WV	129,660	18,902	15%	31	46%	57	36
Cumberland, MD-WV	103,275	19,258	19%	13	31%	75	37
Ithaca, NY	101,540	6,913	7%	80	100%	8	38
Ocean City, NJ	97,229	22,385	23%	7	22%	82	39
Las Cruces, NM	209,197	27,570	13%	38	47%	55	40
Dalton, GA	142,155	16,644	12%	46	50%	48	41
Michigan City-La Porte, IN	111,434	12,247	11%	52	53%	42	42
Johnson City, TN	198,672	15,608	8%	65	58%	32	43
Springfield, OH	138,326	6,578	5%	87	91%	10	44

Table A-2.4: LSA Figures for Metro Areas with Populations Less Than 250,000

Geography	Total Population	Total LSA Population	Total % of Pop in LSA	Rank for Total % of Pop in LSA	% of LSA Pop in Low-Income Area	Rank for % of LSA Pop in Low-Income Area	Composite Rank
Bay City, MI	107,768	12,278	11%	54	53%	43	45
Vineland-Millville-Bridgeton, NJ	156,853	22,260	14%	34	39%	65	46
Jackson, MI	160,247	13,556	8%	70	60%	31	47
Albany, GA	157,266	7,676	5%	86	80%	17	48
Jackson, TN	115,444	5,319	5%	90	85%	13	49
Anderson, SC	187,078	14,081	8%	67	53%	37	50
Jefferson City, MO	149,777	4,364	3%	100	100%	5	51
Weirton-Steubenville, WV-OH	124,384	14,272	11%	51	48%	54	52
Terre Haute, IN	172,335	14,196	8%	68	53%	39	53
Valdosta, GA	139,548	4,847	3%	101	100%	6	54
Champaign-Urbana, IL	231,788	5,016	2%	107	100%	2	55
Waterloo-Cedar Falls, IA	167,810	13,994	8%	69	53%	40	56
Grand Forks, ND-MN	98,443	13,070	13%	43	39%	66	57
Muncie, IN	117,632	6,083	5%	89	74%	21	58
Fargo, ND-MN	208,759	37,454	18%	14	8%	98	59
Oshkosh-Neenah, WI	166,973	20,484	12%	45	38%	67	60
Sherman-Denison, TX	120,831	20,430	17%	20	13%	92	61
Barnstable Town, MA	215,802	27,589	13%	36	28%	77	62
Lake Havasu City-Kingman, AZ	200,146	16,932	8%	64	49%	50	63
Danville, VA	106,533	17,498	16%	25	14%	89	64
St. George, UT	138,092	23,881	17%	18	9%	97	65
Rocky Mount, NC	152,352	3,104	2%	113	100%	4	66
Flagstaff, AZ	134,386	15,723	12%	47	35%	70	67
Burlington, NC	151,088	24,150	16%	23	9%	96	68
Wausau, WI	133,940	17,217	13%	39	26%	80	69
Gainesville, GA	179,645	26,565	15%	27	10%	94	70
Salisbury, MD	125,195	9,781	8%	72	49%	51	71
Goldsboro, NC	122,598	9,181	7%	79	52%	44	72
Wenatchee, WA	110,850	5,279	5%	91	55%	35	73
Sumter, SC	107,421	1,916	2%	119	100%	7	74
Florence, SC	205,495	14,989	7%	75	48%	53	75
Battle Creek, MI	136,146	10,554	8%	71	45%	58	76
Parkersburg-Marietta, WV-OH	162,002	21,938	14%	33	8%	99	77
Sandusky, OH	77,075	9,752	13%	44	14%	90	78
Winchester, VA-WV	128,434	15,544	12%	48	17%	87	79
Danville, IL	81,595	7,225	9%	61	33%	74	80
Fort Walton Beach-Crestview-Destin, FL	180,789	4,649	3%	98	53%	38	81
Bangor, ME	153,856	3,185	2%	112	62%	28	82
Panama City-Lynn Haven, FL	168,822	17,928	11%	50	13%	91	83
Yuma, AZ	195,725	13,153	7%	76	36%	68	84
Victoria, TX	115,372	10,440	9%	60	20%	84	85
Wichita Falls, TX	151,306	3,152	2%	114	58%	33	86
Cleveland, TN	115,757	2,256	2%	118	55%	34	87
Rochester, MN	185,939	10,456	6%	81	29%	76	88

Table A-2.4: LSA Figures for Metro Areas with Populations Less Than 250,000

Geography	Total Population	Total LSA Population	Total % of Pop in LSA	Rank for Total % of Pop in LSA	% of LSA Pop in Low-Income Area	Rank for % of LSA Pop in Low-Income Area	Composite Rank
Prescott, AZ	210,918	20,756	10%	56	0%	102	89
La Crosse, WI-MN	133,613	16,996	13%	40	0%	118	90
Bellingham, WA	201,100	19,447	10%	57	0%	104	91
Texarkana, TX-Texarkana, AR	136,008	9,615	7%	78	21%	83	92
Chico, CA	220,002	9,111	4%	92	34%	71	93
Pascagoula, MS	162,227	11,061	7%	77	14%	88	94
Williamsport, PA	116,079	3,189	3%	105	44%	60	95
Lebanon, PA	133,505	5,084	4%	94	34%	72	96
Longview, WA	102,379	13,479	13%	42	0%	127	97
Johnstown, PA	143,592	8,394	6%	82	10%	95	98
Missoula, MT	109,273	12,498	11%	53	0%	125	99
Tyler, TX	209,651	3,924	2%	108	33%	73	100
Lake Charles, LA	199,595	1,055	1%	121	39%	64	101
Burlington-South Burlington, VT	211,228	10,896	5%	85	0%	101	102
Monroe, MI	152,016	6,432	4%	93	12%	93	103
Coeur d'Alene, ID	138,470	4,732	3%	102	18%	86	104
Glens Falls, NY	128,892	4,330	3%	103	19%	85	105
Great Falls, MT	81,295	7,275	9%	62	0%	130	106
Appleton, WI	225,582	7,167	3%	96	0%	100	107
Bloomington, IN	192,657	5,345	3%	97	0%	106	108
Odessa, TX	137,081	7,522	5%	88	0%	115	109
Elizabethtown, KY	119,725	7,489	6%	83	0%	122	110
Blacksburg-Christiansburg-Radford, VA	162,899	4,993	3%	99	0%	109	111
Elkhart-Goshen, IN	197,478	4,772	2%	109	0%	105	112
Joplin, MO	175,499	3,664	2%	110	0%	108	113
Medford, OR	203,143	2,251	1%	120	0%	103	114
State College, PA	153,953	3,567	2%	111	0%	112	115
Kokomo, IN	98,665	4,434	4%	95	0%	129	116
St. Joseph, MO-KS	127,319	3,812	3%	104	0%	121	117
Morristown, TN	136,574	2,602	2%	115	0%	116	118
Punta Gorda, FL	159,961	2,286	1%	122	0%	110	119
Bismarck, ND	108,745	3,111	3%	106	0%	126	120
Bend, OR	157,697	1,533	1%	123	0%	111	121
Anderson, IN	131,598	2,238	2%	116	0%	119	122
Redding, CA	177,217	688	0%	130	0%	107	123
Auburn-Opelika, AL	140,127	1,393	1%	124	0%	113	124
Sebastian-Vero Beach, FL	137,994	2,013	1%	125	0%	114	125
Mount Vernon-Anacortes, WA	116,875	2,488	2%	117	0%	123	126
Napa, CA	136,524	1,943	1%	126	0%	117	127
Pittsfield, MA	131,161	708	1%	127	0%	120	128
Sheboygan, WI	115,476	1,421	1%	128	0%	124	129
Pine Bluff, AR	100,210	556	1%	129	0%	128	130

Table A-2.5: LSA Figures for Micropolitan Areas

Geography	Total Population	Population in LSA	% of Pop in LSA	Rank for % of Pop in LSA	% of LSA Pop in Low-Income Area	Rank for % of LSA Pop in Low-Income Area	Composite Rank
Amsterdam, NY	50,215	18,152	36%	9	58%	31	1
Macomb, IL	32,604	8,045	25%	39	87%	15	2
Clarksdale, MS	26,140	9,216	35%	13	48%	47	3
Tallulah, LA	12,091	3,080	25%	40	69%	23	4
Gallup, NM	71,476	39,824	56%	2	40%	63	5
Marion, OH	66,490	17,266	26%	32	55%	38	6
Ottumwa, IA	35,611	8,117	23%	46	59%	30	7
Sierra Vista-Douglas, AZ	131,299	30,887	24%	41	54%	40	8
Price, UT	21,396	7,548	35%	14	39%	69	9
New Castle, PA	91,095	24,911	27%	28	43%	56	10
Greenville, MS	51,113	9,441	18%	71	81%	19	11
Austin, MN	39,152	11,867	30%	21	38%	72	12
Los Alamos, NM	17,943	7,942	44%	5	30%	89	13
Somerset, PA	77,724	26,247	34%	15	32%	83	14
Payson, AZ	53,575	11,875	22%	50	47%	49	15
Taos, NM	32,925	13,421	41%	6	28%	93	16
De Ridder, LA	35,646	10,771	30%	22	31%	86	17
Helena-West Helena, AR	21,697	7,880	36%	11	26%	97	18
Cortland, NY	49,322	11,124	23%	45	40%	65	19
Cordele, GA	23,432	4,794	20%	61	46%	52	20
Zanesville, OH	86,039	17,153	20%	55	41%	60	21
Fairmont, WV	56,389	8,475	15%	83	57%	32	22
Bonham, TX	33,907	11,035	33%	17	25%	99	23
Willimantic, CT	118,398	20,945	18%	69	47%	48	24
Rio Grande City, TX	60,955	39,477	65%	1	18%	117	25
Butte-Silver Bow, MT	34,181	6,207	18%	72	48%	46	26
Bay City, TX	36,689	4,273	12%	112	100%	7	27
Minot, ND	69,537	17,951	26%	31	29%	90	28
Marinette, WI-MI	65,772	15,286	23%	43	34%	80	29
Oneonta, NY	62,246	12,394	20%	57	39%	67	30
Key West, FL	73,041	22,298	31%	18	20%	107	31
Lake City, FL	67,516	19,951	30%	19	20%	108	32
Klamath Falls, OR	66,349	14,765	22%	48	34%	79	33
Uvalde, TX	26,396	7,261	28%	27	25%	100	34
Selma, AL	43,804	5,812	13%	100	59%	29	35
Harrisburg, IL	24,912	4,781	19%	67	41%	62	36
Deming, NM	25,087	2,944	12%	113	82%	17	37
Greenwood, SC	69,661	9,072	13%	96	55%	37	38
Vicksburg, MS	48,760	14,298	29%	24	20%	109	39
Ardmore, OK	56,967	14,844	26%	33	23%	102	40
Greenwood, MS	42,899	5,508	13%	101	57%	34	41
Pittsburg, KS	39,118	5,061	13%	103	57%	35	42
Morgan City, LA	54,645	10,664	20%	58	33%	81	43
Wauchula, FL	27,724	2,668	10%	128	100%	11	44

Table A-2.5: LSA Figures for Micropolitan Areas

Geography	Total Population	Population in LSA	% of Pop in LSA	Rank for % of Pop in LSA	% of LSA Pop in Low-Income Area	Rank for % of LSA Pop in Low-Income Area	Composite Rank
Pierre Part, LA	23,421	9,548	41%	7	13%	132	45
Liberal, KS	22,944	5,121	22%	51	30%	88	46
Beckley, WV	78,837	14,146	18%	70	38%	70	47
Elizabeth City, NC	64,078	13,055	20%	56	32%	84	48
Cornelia, GA	43,041	4,731	11%	119	70%	22	49
Kill Devil Hills, NC	33,913	6,481	19%	65	36%	76	50
Pahrump, NV	43,907	23,516	54%	3	10%	139	51
Oak Harbor, WA	78,494	19,351	25%	38	21%	106	52
Havre, MT	16,090	3,508	22%	52	28%	94	53
Espanola, NM	40,232	19,721	49%	4	8%	143	54
Big Rapids, MI	42,797	5,800	14%	91	43%	57	55
Astoria, OR	37,039	13,966	38%	8	10%	140	56
Martinsville, VA	67,952	19,973	29%	23	15%	126	57
Meridian, MS	107,412	11,620	11%	115	56%	36	58
Wilson, NC	81,218	6,735	8%	148	100%	3	59
Corning, NY	98,952	8,533	9%	132	72%	21	60
Hudson, NY	63,077	7,472	12%	108	48%	45	61
Sikeston, MO	39,174	14,298	36%	10	7%	144	62
Plattsburgh, NY	82,109	20,687	25%	37	17%	120	63
Lexington Park, MD	105,145	28,996	28%	25	12%	133	64
Adrian, MI	99,888	10,754	11%	116	53%	42	65
Palatka, FL	74,340	14,309	19%	62	26%	96	66
Chambersburg, PA	149,575	17,509	12%	105	44%	55	67
Helena, MT	74,797	6,628	9%	134	67%	26	68
Elko, NV	50,794	10,329	20%	59	23%	103	69
Grants, NM	27,210	2,079	8%	154	100%	12	70
Homosassa Springs, FL	141,196	33,175	23%	42	14%	127	71
Ashtabula, OH	101,497	7,990	8%	145	67%	25	72
Oak Hill, WV	46,016	3,998	9%	138	57%	33	73
Sevierville, TN	89,872	22,397	25%	36	10%	138	74
Carbondale, IL	60,204	6,003	10%	125	46%	51	75
Middlesborough, KY	28,686	5,643	20%	60	19%	116	76
Centralia, WA	75,430	13,013	17%	73	22%	104	77
Cleveland, MS	34,134	2,499	7%	164	82%	16	78
Pecos, TX	13,777	975	7%	167	100%	14	79
Clearlake, CA	64,659	13,904	22%	49	12%	134	80
Bogalusa, LA	47,168	6,130	13%	98	32%	85	81
Gardnerville Ranchos, NV	46,986	8,153	17%	75	20%	110	82
Harrison, AR	45,216	2,178	5%	183	100%	6	83
Shelton, WA	60,681	21,353	35%	12	0%	178	84
Granbury, TX	59,671	6,689	11%	117	37%	74	85
Mount Sterling, KY	44,386	7,710	17%	77	19%	114	86
Ada, OK	37,475	4,903	13%	104	30%	87	87
Port Angeles, WA	71,383	6,091	9%	135	42%	58	88

Table A-2.5: LSA Figures for Micropolitan Areas

Geography	Total Population	Population in LSA	% of Pop in LSA	Rank for % of Pop in LSA	% of LSA Pop in Low-Income Area	Rank for % of LSA Pop in Low-Income Area	Composite Rank
Cedar City, UT	46,158	7,462	16%	82	20%	112	89
Muscatine, IA	54,107	4,963	9%	136	42%	59	90
Hilton Head Island-Beaufort, SC	186,977	10,702	6%	168	61%	28	91
Wahpeton, ND-MN	22,894	3,788	17%	79	18%	118	92
Morehead City, NC	66,449	8,075	12%	107	29%	91	93
Crescent City, CA	28,610	1,373	5%	189	100%	10	94
Palestine, TX	58,438	17,374	30%	20	0%	180	95
Roswell, NM	65,632	11,400	17%	74	14%	128	96
Brookings, OR	22,358	1,029	5%	191	100%	13	97
Norfolk, NE	48,259	9,244	19%	63	9%	142	98
Seneca, SC	74,253	11,780	16%	81	15%	125	99
Watertown-Fort Drum, NY	116,203	16,767	14%	90	16%	121	100
Jamestown-Dunkirk-Fredonia, NY	134,863	5,129	4%	195	81%	18	101
Coldwater, MI	45,247	7,895	17%	76	11%	137	102
Fort Polk South, LA	52,319	14,334	27%	29	0%	185	103
Natchez, MS-LA	53,103	3,336	6%	175	54%	41	104
Bemidji, MN	44,428	3,499	8%	150	39%	68	105
Ottawa-Streator, IL	154,951	12,344	8%	142	34%	77	106
Calhoun, GA	55,173	1,407	3%	215	100%	4	107
La Grande, OR	25,736	3,915	15%	89	13%	131	108
McComb, MS	53,517	1,913	4%	201	73%	20	109
Lewistown, PA	46,668	13,070	28%	26	0%	195	110
Sebring, FL	98,755	5,863	6%	169	45%	53	111
Rockland, ME	39,721	13,460	34%	16	0%	207	112
East Stroudsburg, PA	169,806	27,099	16%	80	5%	145	113
Crossville, TN	56,045	12,830	23%	44	0%	181	114
Kearney, NE	51,024	3,555	7%	162	40%	64	115
Muskogee, OK	70,957	2,651	4%	200	62%	27	116
Cullman, AL	80,387	9,666	12%	106	16%	122	117
Stillwater, OK	77,333	5,631	7%	158	38%	71	118
Truckee-Grass Valley, CA	98,738	2,198	2%	229	100%	1	119
Manitowoc, WI	81,418	5,177	6%	171	41%	61	120
Marion-Herrin, IL	66,328	8,378	13%	97	9%	141	121
Hastings, NE	37,906	1,721	5%	186	45%	54	122
The Villages, FL	93,410	3,913	4%	198	51%	44	123
Oxford, MS	47,343	1,155	2%	240	100%	5	124
Alice, TX	40,825	2,686	7%	163	33%	82	125
East Liverpool-Salem, OH	107,840	4,630	4%	196	46%	50	126
Safford, AZ	45,644	5,250	12%	110	11%	136	127
Mankato-North Mankato, MN	96,715	7,901	8%	146	24%	101	128
Madisonville, KY	46,908	4,355	9%	137	20%	111	129
Grants Pass, OR	82,687	1,214	1%	250	100%	2	130
McAlester, OK	45,816	4,128	9%	139	20%	113	131
Eufaula, AL-GA	29,961	471	2%	243	100%	9	132

Table A-2.5: LSA Figures for Micropolitan Areas

Geography	Total Population	Population in LSA	% of Pop in LSA	Rank for % of Pop in LSA	% of LSA Pop in Low-Income Area	Rank for % of LSA Pop in Low-Income Area	Composite Rank
Phoenix Lake-Cedar Ridge, CA	55,341	2,700	5%	181	36%	75	133
Danville, KY	53,185	5,294	10%	126	13%	130	134
Batavia, NY	60,063	1,646	3%	214	52%	43	135
Arkadelphia, AR	22,988	1,709	7%	166	29%	92	136
Aberdeen, WA	72,768	9,565	13%	95	0%	166	137
Cambridge, MD	32,618	8,349	26%	34	0%	228	138
Kingsville, TX	32,470	416	1%	256	100%	8	139
Thomasville-Lexington, NC	162,832	14,972	9%	130	11%	135	140
Pottsville, PA	148,217	2,857	2%	227	54%	39	141
Moses Lake, WA	89,108	6,710	8%	147	17%	119	142
El Dorado, AR	41,622	3,369	8%	151	19%	115	143
Augusta-Waterville, ME	122,116	9,481	8%	144	15%	123	144
Lebanon, NH-VT	174,696	2,082	1%	247	67%	24	145
Paris, TX	49,793	7,297	15%	84	0%	188	146
City of The Dalles, OR	25,203	6,793	27%	30	0%	242	147
Wooster, OH	114,525	11,030	10%	122	0%	151	148
Eureka-Arcata-Fortuna, CA	134,623	4,143	3%	209	39%	66	149
Susanville, CA	34,894	7,333	21%	53	0%	222	150
Roseburg, OR	107,622	11,181	10%	123	0%	153	151
Indiana, PA	88,878	3,405	4%	199	34%	78	152
Brookings, SD	31,965	7,208	23%	47	0%	230	153
Gettysburg, PA	101,362	10,259	10%	124	0%	154	154
Rock Springs, WY	43,795	7,311	17%	78	0%	200	155
Traverse City, MI	143,365	12,409	9%	131	0%	148	156
Watertown, SD	33,129	6,948	21%	54	0%	225	157
Whitewater, WI	102,209	6,878	7%	157	15%	124	158
Coshocton, OH	36,901	7,166	19%	64	0%	217	159
Raymondville, TX	22,128	5,774	26%	35	0%	248	160
Bozeman, MT	89,493	3,076	3%	211	37%	73	161
Bluefield, WV-VA	107,297	7,735	7%	156	13%	129	162
Greeneville, TN	68,803	3,344	5%	180	22%	105	163
Fort Madison-Keokuk, IA-MO	42,985	6,442	15%	85	0%	202	164
Sunbury, PA	94,508	3,525	4%	197	27%	95	165
Ukiah, CA	87,821	7,468	9%	133	0%	159	166
Harriman, TN	54,164	6,621	12%	109	0%	183	167
Manhattan, KS	127,048	10,593	8%	143	0%	150	168
Selinsgrove, PA	39,690	5,763	15%	86	0%	208	169
Huntingdon, PA	45,887	5,802	13%	99	0%	197	170
Miami, OK	31,837	6,127	19%	66	0%	231	171
Minden, LA	41,189	5,408	13%	102	0%	204	172
Newport, TN	35,651	5,449	15%	87	0%	221	173
Culpeper, VA	46,684	5,190	11%	118	0%	194	174
Burley, ID	43,012	5,092	12%	111	0%	201	175
Brigham City, UT	49,962	1,625	3%	217	25%	98	176

Table A-2.5: LSA Figures for Micropolitan Areas

Geography	Total Population	Population in LSA	% of Pop in LSA	Rank for % of Pop in LSA	% of LSA Pop in Low-Income Area	Rank for % of LSA Pop in Low-Income Area	Composite Rank
Woodward, OK	20,076	3,832	19%	68	0%	254	177
Grand Island, NE	72,708	4,829	7%	159	0%	167	178
Great Bend, KS	27,659	4,104	15%	88	0%	238	179
Lumberton, NC	134,138	7,102	5%	179	0%	149	180
Galesburg, IL	70,605	4,693	7%	160	0%	168	181
Mineral Wells, TX	28,111	4,060	14%	92	0%	236	182
Pendleton-Hermiston, OR	87,034	5,518	6%	170	0%	160	183
Athens, OH	64,755	4,746	7%	161	0%	172	184
Lancaster, SC	76,636	4,257	6%	172	0%	163	185
Scottsbluff, NE	37,645	4,223	11%	120	0%	215	186
Marshfield-Wisconsin Rapids, WI	74,721	4,800	6%	173	0%	165	187
Plymouth, IN	47,034	3,791	8%	149	0%	192	188
Forest City, NC	67,791	3,997	6%	174	0%	169	189
Jamestown, ND	21,100	2,931	14%	93	0%	250	190
Guymon, OK	20,635	2,939	14%	94	0%	252	191
Brevard, NC	33,080	3,408	10%	127	0%	226	192
Dickinson, ND	24,982	2,980	12%	114	0%	243	193
Garden City, KS	36,776	3,309	9%	140	0%	219	194
Twin Falls, ID	99,577	2,834	3%	210	0%	155	195
Stephenville, TX	37,889	3,054	8%	152	0%	214	196
Clinton, IA	49,104	2,407	5%	182	0%	190	197
Gillette, WY	46,124	2,578	6%	176	0%	196	198
Findlay, OH	74,781	1,904	3%	212	0%	164	199
Borger, TX	22,142	2,242	10%	129	0%	247	200
Pella, IA	33,299	2,763	8%	153	0%	224	201
Huron, SD	17,398	1,999	11%	121	0%	257	202
Ogdensburg-Massena, NY	111,909	2,470	2%	228	0%	152	203
La Follette, TN	40,699	2,522	6%	177	0%	205	204
Duncan, OK	45,031	2,091	5%	184	0%	199	205
Cape Girardeau-Jackson, MO-IL	96,242	1,456	2%	230	0%	156	206
Brainerd, MN	91,008	2,039	2%	231	0%	157	207
Kalispell, MT	90,902	1,442	2%	232	0%	158	208
Torrington, CT	189,854	2,732	1%	246	0%	146	209
Georgetown, SC	60,169	1,670	3%	213	0%	179	210
Natchitoches, LA	39,550	2,167	5%	185	0%	209	211
Boone, IA	26,295	2,051	8%	155	0%	240	212
Bishop, CA	18,546	1,583	9%	141	0%	256	213
Las Vegas, NM	29,382	2,050	7%	165	0%	235	214
Fernley, NV	51,973	1,676	3%	216	0%	186	215
Daphne-Fairhope, AL	182,225	544	0%	257	0%	147	216
Charleston-Mattoon, IL	64,909	1,394	2%	233	0%	171	217
Durant, OK	42,403	1,565	4%	202	0%	203	218
Newton, IA	36,831	1,983	5%	187	0%	218	219
Hobbs, NM	64,702	1,402	2%	234	0%	173	220

Table A-2.5: LSA Figures for Micropolitan Areas

Geography	Total Population	Population in LSA	% of Pop in LSA	Rank for % of Pop in LSA	% of LSA Pop in Low-Income Area	Rank for % of LSA Pop in Low-Income Area	Composite Rank
Branson, MO	83,860	836	1%	248	0%	161	221
Washington, NC	47,743	1,355	3%	218	0%	191	222
Coos Bay, OR	63,015	997	2%	235	0%	175	223
Opelousas-Eunice, LA	83,379	769	1%	249	0%	162	224
Lock Haven, PA	39,228	1,466	4%	203	0%	210	225
Pontiac, IL	38,831	1,495	4%	204	0%	211	226
Henderson, NC	45,413	1,542	3%	219	0%	198	227
Gloversville, NY	55,507	1,200	2%	236	0%	182	228
Marshall, TX	65,609	984	1%	251	0%	170	229
Ontario, OR-ID	53,928	823	2%	237	0%	184	230
Lincoln, IL	30,290	1,627	5%	188	0%	233	231
Malone, NY	51,587	895	2%	238	0%	187	232
Alamogordo, NM	63,779	544	1%	252	0%	174	233
Okeechobee, FL	39,985	1,265	3%	220	0%	206	234
Kerrville, TX	49,623	748	2%	239	0%	189	235
Ruston, LA	62,995	939	1%	253	0%	176	236
Mountain Home, ID	27,030	1,455	5%	190	0%	239	237
Fremont, OH	60,925	599	1%	254	0%	177	238
Troy, AL	32,838	1,436	4%	205	0%	227	239
Portales, NM	19,842	1,163	6%	178	0%	255	240
Canon City, CO	46,808	808	2%	241	0%	193	241
Sault Ste. Marie, MI	38,512	1,158	3%	221	0%	213	242
North Platte, NE	37,575	1,302	3%	222	0%	216	243
Hood River, OR	22,342	1,153	5%	192	0%	246	244
Silver City, NM	29,512	1,065	4%	206	0%	234	245
Tuskegee, AL	21,443	1,024	5%	193	0%	249	246
Laramie, WY	36,288	1,046	3%	223	0%	220	247
Yazoo City, MS	28,055	1,197	4%	207	0%	237	248
Fairmont, MN	20,829	1,067	5%	194	0%	251	249
Dodge City, KS	33,837	1,061	3%	224	0%	223	250
Mitchell, SD	22,834	930	4%	208	0%	244	251
Camden, AR	31,470	930	3%	225	0%	232	252
Houghton, MI	38,779	442	1%	255	0%	212	253
Mount Pleasant, TX	32,333	695	2%	242	0%	229	254
Ruidoso, NM	20,490	547	3%	226	0%	253	255
Marshall, MN	25,845	614	2%	244	0%	241	256
Williston, ND	22,395	538	2%	245	0%	245	257

low-income burden and much lower values for relative size, such as Calhoun, GA; Oxford, MS and Grants Pass, OR.

All Core-Based Statistical Areas

Figure A-2 shows a scatter plot of the percentage of population living in LSA areas and the percentage of LSA-area population living in low-income block groups for all CBSAs listed in the above tables—metropolitan areas (grouped by

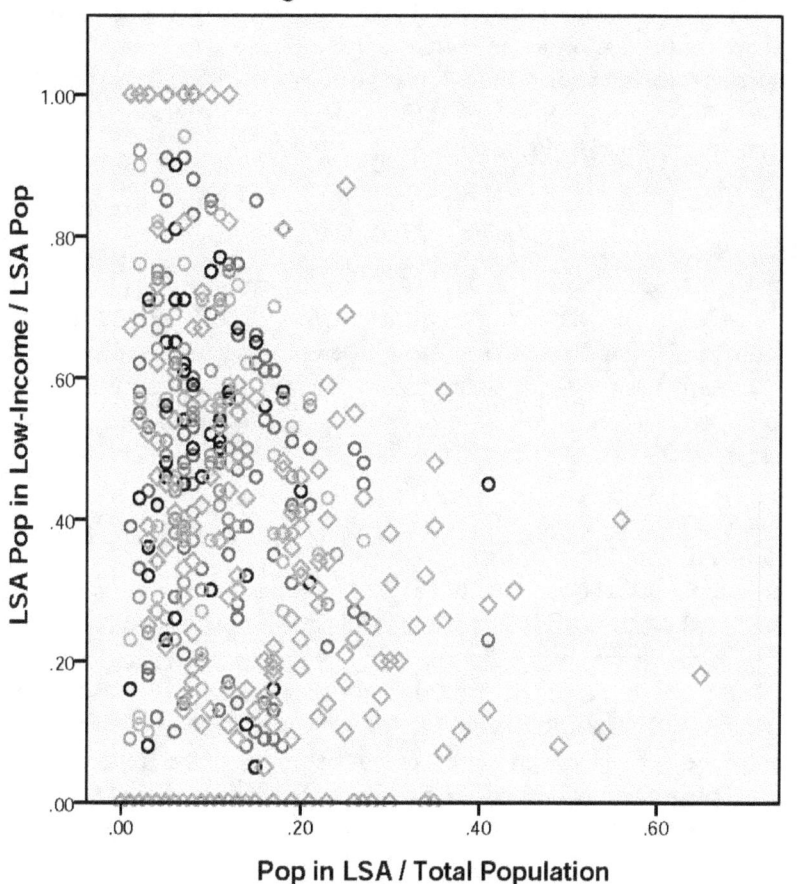

Figure A-2: LSA Scatter Plot for CBSAs

size) and micropolitan areas. None of the population groups shows a significant correlation between the two variables.

Census Places (Cities and Towns)

Cities with Populations Greater than 500,000

The average large city with a population greater than 500,000 has 13% of its population living in LSAs, 65% of which lives in low-income areas. Table A-3.1 ranks cities with populations greater than 500,000, with Washington, DC ranked first, followed by Baltimore, Philadelphia, Dallas and Milwaukee in the top five. Jacksonville and Charlotte exhibit interesting figures in that their values for relative size are well below the 13% average at 6% and 4% (27th and 29th rank) while being well above the average low-income burden of 65% (86% and 87%, or 6th and 5th rank, respectively). Even though these two cities do not have an overwhelming percentage of their populations living in LSAs, the concentration of that population in low-income areas is remarkably high. Fort Worth shows the opposite relationship between the two variables, being ranked first and 31st (31% and 36%).

Cities with Populations of 250,000 to 500,000

The average city with a population between 250,000 and 500,000 has 16% of its population living in LSAs, 68% of which lives in low-income areas. Table A-3.2 ranks cities with populations between 250,000 and 500,000, with Cleveland exhibiting high percentages for both variables (top 10 rankings in each), followed by Kansas City, St. Louis, Newark and Buffalo in the top five. Excepting Cleveland, this population group's top five tend to have one highly ranked variable coupled with a moderately ranked variable, such as Kansas City and Newark, where relative size and low-income burden are ranked 18th/first and 16th/third, respectively.

Cities with Populations of 100,000 to 250,000

The average city with a population between 100,000 and 250,000 has 14% of its population living in LSAs, 63% of which lives in low-income areas. Table A-3.3 lists the top 10, middle 10, and bottom 10 cities with populations between 100,000 and 250,000 based on their composite rankings. Richmond, VA is ranked first, followed by Knoxville, Syracuse, Baton Rouge and New Haven, CT in the top five. Several cities in the middle 10 rankings have a notably high percentage value in low-income burden: Spokane, WA; Eugene, OR; Glendale, AZ and Little Rock, AR have values of either 100% or above 89% for low-income burden yet have remarkably low values for the relative size of the problem, ranging from 1% to 6%. Even if a financing program is interested in prioritizing areas based on the extent to which LSA residents live in low-income areas, these serve as examples of cities for which the populations living in LSAs is simply too small to warrant significant intervention.

Cities with Populations of 50,000 to 100,000

The average city with a population between 50,000 and 100,000 has 17% of its population living in LSAs, 51% of which lives in low-income areas. Table A-3.4 lists the top 10, middle 10 and bottom 10 cities with populations between 50,000 and 100,000 based on their composite rankings. Camden, NJ is ranked first, followed by Trenton, NJ; Gary, IN; Lawrence, MA and Youngstown, OH in the top five. All cities in the top 10 show an overwhelming need for improved access to full-service supermarkets, with sizeable populations in LSAs and a significant concentration of LSA population in low-income areas (80% or more). Like the 100,000 to 250,000 population group, several cities in the middle 10 rankings show a notably high percentage of LSA population in low-income areas: Scranton, PA; Jackson, TN and Wichita Fall, TX have values of either 100% or above 84% for low-income burden yet have notably low values for relative size, ranging from 2% to 9%. These also serve as examples of cities in which the populations living in LSAs is simply too small to warrant significant intervention.

Cities with Populations of Less than 50,000

The average city with a population of less than 50,000 has 68% of its population living in LSAs, 42% of which lives in low-income areas. Table A-3.5 lists the top 10, middle 10 and bottom 10 cities with populations of less than 50,000 based on their composite rankings. Because many of these cities are small enough to be entirely within a single LSA, the top 10 cities all have 100% values for both variables, which mitigates the rankings' significance. Only in the middle 10 rankings do we see more realistic rankings among these cities, although they do not appear to be in need of food-access

Table A-3.1: LSA Figures for Cities with Populations of More Than 500,000

Geography	State	Total Population	Poplulation in LSA	% of Pop in LSA	Rank for % of Pop in LSA	% of LSA Pop in Low-Income Area	Rank for % of LSA Pop in Low-Income Area	Composite Rank
Washington	District of Columbia	601,722	143,167	24%	4	91%	2	1
Baltimore	Maryland	620,956	184,075	30%	2	86%	7	2
Philadelphia	Pennsylvania	1,525,931	324,927	21%	7	85%	8	3
Dallas	Texas	1,222,935	203,339	17%	11	87%	4	4
Milwaukee	Wisconsin	594,651	136,412	23%	6	81%	11	5
Detroit	Michigan	713,753	165,492	23%	5	75%	13	6
Memphis	Tennessee	646,247	134,632	21%	8	82%	10	7
Boston	Massachusetts	616,850	152,765	25%	3	61%	20	8
Nashville	Tennessee	598,704	56,155	9%	22	90%	3	9
Louisville	Kentucky	607,255	45,326	7%	25	95%	1	10
Chicago	Illinois	2,696,355	337,662	13%	15	74%	14	11
Columbus	Ohio	728,550	116,994	16%	13	64%	17	12
San Francisco	California	805,222	79,589	10%	20	77%	12	13
Fort Worth	Texas	726,044	226,549	31%	1	36%	31	14
Denver	Colorado	600,088	72,645	12%	16	71%	16	15
Los Angeles	California	3,781,978	280,635	7%	24	82%	9	16
Houston	Texas	2,139,942	327,515	15%	14	61%	19	17
San Antonio	Texas	1,334,214	273,197	20%	9	54%	24	18
Jacksonville	Florida	822,850	47,485	6%	27	86%	6	19
Charlotte	North Carolina	694,752	28,652	4%	29	87%	5	20
Austin	Texas	758,449	128,523	17%	12	58%	23	21
El Paso	Texas	635,829	59,394	9%	21	63%	18	22
Tucson	Arizona	529,581	95,840	18%	10	44%	29	23
Phoenix	Arizona	1,448,771	138,801	10%	19	59%	22	24
Indianapolis	Indiana	822,872	92,180	11%	17	50%	25	25
Oklahoma	Oklahoma	587,382	66,561	11%	18	45%	28	26
Portland	Oregon	584,689	8,933	2%	33	73%	15	27
New York	New York	8,174,970	363,761	4%	28	60%	21	28
Las Vegas	Nevada	543,420	36,360	7%	26	48%	27	29
San Diego	California	1,266,610	41,023	3%	30	48%	26	30
Albuquerque	New Mexico	512,237	42,680	8%	23	10%	33	31
Seattle	Washington	608,605	12,686	2%	32	43%	30	32
San Jose	California	892,346	16,550	2%	31	12%	32	33

Table A-3.2: LSA Figures for Cities with Populations Between 250,000 and 500,000

Geography	State	Total Population	Population in LSA	% of Pop in LSA	Rank for % of Pop in LSA	% of LSA Pop in Low-Income Area	Rank for % of LSA Pop in Low-Income Area	Composite Rank
Cleveland	Ohio	396,845	88,272	22%	8	93%	4	1
Kansas City	Missouri	459,733	41,009	9%	18	97%	1	2
St. Louis	Missouri	318,905	130,200	41%	4	78%	15	3
Newark	New Jersey	276,609	34,807	13%	16	95%	3	4
Buffalo	New York	261,369	93,680	36%	5	77%	16	5
Tulsa	Oklahoma	388,667	42,289	11%	17	89%	5	6
Bakersfield	California	313,314	26,705	9%	20	97%	2	7
Pittsburgh	Pennsylvania	305,965	145,245	47%	2	71%	21	8
Cincinnati	Ohio	301,177	137,516	46%	3	72%	20	9
St. Paul	Minnesota	285,087	49,198	17%	12	79%	11	10
Minneapolis	Minnesota	382,402	78,386	20%	9	74%	18	11
New Orleans	Louisiana	343,815	177,282	52%	1	63%	27	12
Wichita	Kansas	353,948	52,178	15%	15	78%	14	13
Atlanta	Georgia	425,438	150,061	35%	6	67%	24	14
Miami	Florida	402,141	59,354	15%	14	75%	17	15
Stockton	California	254,622	17,156	7%	23	84%	8	16
Raleigh	North Carolina	331,932	17,770	5%	26	89%	6	17
Greensboro	North Carolina	251,511	23,382	9%	21	79%	12	18
Colorado Springs	Colorado	414,688	22,996	6%	24	80%	10	19
Lexington	Kentucky	295,769	53,010	18%	11	70%	23	20
Oakland	California	392,028	17,038	4%	28	88%	7	21
Tampa	Florida	338,909	65,751	19%	10	67%	25	22
Corpus Christi	Texas	302,141	94,912	31%	7	43%	30	23
Omaha	Nebraska	392,898	14,216	4%	27	78%	13	24
Toledo	Ohio	285,154	45,550	16%	13	55%	28	25
Mesa	Arizona	428,105	8,667	2%	33	82%	9	26
Sacramento	California	428,549	29,293	7%	22	70%	22	27
Fresno	California	459,482	41,387	9%	19	54%	29	28
Long Beach	California	463,334	12,296	3%	30	73%	19	29
Arlington	Texas	377,590	17,162	5%	25	64%	26	30
Aurora	Colorado	312,800	12,272	4%	29	42%	31	31
Anaheim	California	329,625	9,844	3%	31	0%	33	32
Virginia Beach	Virginia	437,794	1,080	0%	34	0%	32	33
Riverside	California	300,489	8,497	3%	32	0%	35	34

Table A-3.3: LSA Figures for Cities with Populations Between 100,000 and 250,000

Top 10 Cities

Geography	State	Total Population	Population in LSA	% of Pop in LSA	Rank for % of Pop in LSA	% of LSA Pop in Low Income Area	Rank for % of LSA Pop in Low Inc	Composite Rank
Richmond	Virginia	204,209	90,593	44%	4	86%	31	1
Knoxville	Tennessee	178,493	31,637	18%	30	100%	6	2
Syracuse	New York	145,045	37,079	26%	15	91%	21	3
Baton Rouge	Louisiana	210,687	62,715	30%	8	85%	34	4
New Haven	Connecticut	129,763	64,460	50%	3	82%	41	5
Rochester	New York	210,480	78,369	37%	5	82%	40	6
Des Moines	Iowa	199,342	30,130	15%	41	100%	4	7
Hartford	Connecticut	124,365	33,984	27%	13	86%	33	8
Savannah	Georgia	137,117	37,041	27%	12	85%	36	9
North Charleston	South Carolina	117,472	24,287	21%	25	90%	24	10

Middle 10 Cities

Geography	State	Total Population	Population in LSA	% of Pop in LSA	Rank for % of Pop in LSA	% of LSA Pop in Low Income Area	Rank for % of LSA Pop in Low Inc	Composite Rank
Spokane	Washington	195,023	6,849	4%	94	100%	5	52
Springfield	Illinois	104,415	24,700	24%	21	47%	83	53
Lancaster	California	159,665	27,911	17%	35	64%	70	54
Eugene	Oregon	142,518	5,306	4%	98	100%	8	55
St. Petersburg	Florida	237,574	38,862	16%	37	63%	71	56
Winston-Salem	North Carolina	223,693	30,413	14%	43	66%	66	57
North Las Vegas	Nevada	215,168	62,163	29%	9	7%	100	58
Glendale	Arizona	222,526	2,907	1%	108	100%	2	59
Paradise CDP	Nevada	217,046	12,702	6%	84	89%	26	60
Little Rock	Arkansas	180,461	6,973	4%	96	95%	16	61

Bottom 10 Cities

Geography	State	Total Population	Population in LSA	% of Pop in LSA	Rank for % of Pop in LSA	% of LSA Pop in Low Income Area	Rank for % of LSA Pop in Low Inc	Composite Rank
Sterling Heights	Michigan	129,698	14,707	11%	56	0%	150	104
Port St. Lucie	Florida	175,520	8,711	5%	89	0%	124	105
Surprise	Arizona	110,790	9,793	9%	71	0%	176	106
Bellevue	Washington	118,912	6,284	5%	93	0%	158	107
Orange	California	125,047	1,222	1%	109	0%	155	108
Rialto	California	101,016	8,624	9%	72	0%	195	109
Gainesville	Florida	114,630	1,051	1%	110	0%	164	110
Norman	Oklahoma	111,185	3,031	3%	103	0%	175	111
Everett	Washington	105,361	3,796	4%	100	0%	186	112
Westminster	Colorado	105,840	2,602	2%	106	0%	185	113

Table A-3.4: LSA Figures for Cities with Populations Between 50,000 and 100,000

Top 10 Places

Geography	State	Total Population	Population in LSA	% of Pop in LSA	Rank for % of Pop in LSA	% of LSA Pop in Low-Income Area	Rank for % of LSA Pop in Low-Income Area	Composite Rank
Camden	New Jersey	77,704	22,737	29%	29	100%	9	1
Trenton	New Jersey	84,891	38,466	45%	7	91%	38	2
Gary	Indiana	80,279	33,562	42%	8	85%	47	3
Lawrence	Massachusetts	76,412	29,252	38%	14	90%	41	4
Youngstown	Ohio	66,862	22,931	34%	19	93%	36	5
Waukegan	Illinois	87,742	41,928	48%	6	84%	50	6
Albany	New York	97,785	46,878	48%	5	83%	53	7
Schenectady	New York	66,499	34,557	52%	3	80%	62	8
Daytona Beach	Florida	53,916	17,210	32%	22	87%	44	9
Decatur	Illinois	64,508	17,301	27%	39	95%	33	10

Middle 10 Places

Geography	State	Total Population	Population in LSA	% of Pop in LSA	Rank for % of Pop in LSA	% of LSA Pop in Low-Income Area	Rank for % of LSA Pop in Low-Income Area	Composite Rank
Scranton	Pennsylvania	76,143	6,892	9%	115	84%	51	86
Albany	Georgia	76,449	7,676	10%	106	80%	61	87
Pawtucket	Rhode Island	71,144	11,255	16%	77	61%	90	88
Waterford	Michigan	71,697	19,623	27%	38	16%	130	89
Jackson	Tennessee	60,989	5,319	9%	122	85%	48	90
Wichita Falls	Texas	95,079	1,839	2%	170	100%	3	91
North Little Rock	Arkansas	62,091	6,018	10%	109	77%	64	92
Stratford	Connecticut	51,372	6,655	13%	88	65%	85	93
Missouri	Texas	62,097	16,583	27%	40	13%	134	94
Baytown	Texas	61,959	9,707	16%	78	53%	97	95

Bottom 10 Places

Geography	State	Total Population	Population in LSA	% of Pop in LSA	Rank for % of Pop in LSA	% of LSA Pop in Low-Income Area	Rank for % of LSA Pop in Low-Income Area	Composite Rank
Apple Valley	California	67,905	1,740	3%	165	0%	275	173
Tinley Park	Illinois	56,064	10,986	20%	63	0%	385	174
Des Plaines	Illinois	62,248	4,601	7%	143	0%	317	175
Yorba Linda	California	55,948	9,450	17%	73	0%	387	176
Edinburg	Texas	56,763	5,721	10%	110	0%	373	177
West Haven	Connecticut	55,485	5,540	10%	111	0%	395	178
Haverhill	Massachusetts	60,869	895	1%	181	0%	329	179
Monterey Park	California	59,999	2,006	3%	167	0%	343	180
Mount Prospect	Illinois	50,078	4,337	9%	127	0%	446	181
Florissant	Missouri	50,018	1,368	3%	169	0%	450	182

Table A-3.5: LSA Figures for Cities with Population Less Than 500,000

Top 10 Places

Geography	State	Total Population	Population in LSA	% of Pop in LSA	Rank for % of Pop in LSA	% of LSA Pop in Low-Income Area	Rank for % of LSA Pop in Low-Income Area	Composite Rank
Holiday-Berkeley	New Jersey	12,710	12,710	100%	11	100%	73	1
Kings Point	Florida	8,288	8,288	100%	41	100%	101	2
Abram-Perezville	Texas	7,910	7,910	100%	45	100%	104	3
Ambridge	Pennsylvania	7,067	7,067	100%	51	100%	111	4
Leisure	New Jersey	6,612	6,612	100%	58	100%	120	5
Century	Florida	6,534	6,534	100%	61	100%	121	6
South Highpoint	Florida	6,348	6,348	100%	65	100%	123	7
Earlimart	California	5,828	5,828	100%	78	100%	128	8
South Bay	Florida	5,424	5,424	100%	84	100%	133	9
Frostburg	Maryland	5,340	5,340	100%	85	100%	134	10

Middle 10 Places

Bristol	Rhode Island	22,985	11,391	50%	936	16%	798	729
North St. Paul	Minnesota	11,618	6,183	53%	915	10%	819	730
Lehi	Utah	47,796	23,948	50%	935	14%	808	731
Falcon Heights	Minnesota	5,321	1,927	36%	1,082	41%	670	732
Socorro	Texas	28,220	12,069	43%	1,004	26%	750	733
Security-Widefield	Colorado	29,524	14,472	49%	944	12%	815	734
DeKalb	Illinois	35,504	4,364	12%	1,348	84%	412	735
Belleville	Illinois	41,377	12,522	30%	1,146	50%	617	736
Carteret	New Jersey	22,802	7,626	33%	1,110	43%	654	737
Drexel Heights	Arizona	30,421	13,849	46%	978	16%	797	738

Bottom 10 Places

Groton Long Point	Connecticut	518	518	100%	687	0%	11,817	1,458
Arcadia	Oklahoma	508	508	100%	690	0%	11,833	1,459
Medicine Park	Oklahoma	491	491	100%	692	0%	11,845	1,460
Rosslyn Farms	Pennsylvania	486	486	100%	694	0%	11,852	1,461
Morgan	Texas	475	475	100%	695	0%	11,870	1,462
Arthur	Nebraska	460	460	100%	698	0%	11,884	1,463
Westhope	North Dakota	446	446	100%	700	0%	11,893	1,464
Mapleton	Pennsylvania	442	442	100%	701	0%	11,895	1,465
Thomaston	Maine	399	399	100%	704	0%	11,916	1,466
Hinton	Oklahoma	358	358	100%	705	0%	11,928	1,467

intervention, as they have either too few LSA residents or a lack of LSA residents living in low-income areas.

All Core-Based Statistical Areas

Figure A-3 shows a scatter plot of the percentages of populations living in LSA areas and the percentages of LSA-area populations living in low-income block groups for all cities of more than 100,000 residents. None of the population groups shows a significant correlation between the two variables.

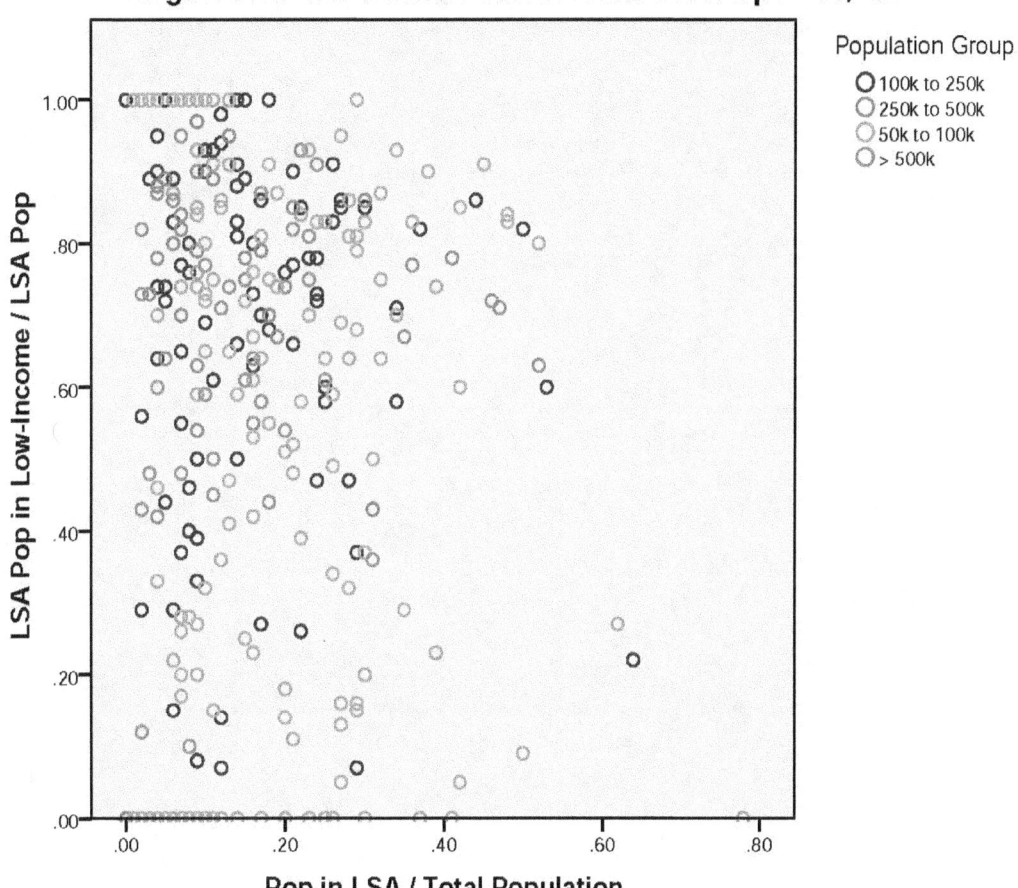

Figure A-3: LSA Scatter Plot for Cities with Pop > 100,000

Appendix 4:
Identifying Optimal Areas for Supermarket Development

Identifying Optimal Areas for
Supermarket Development

Date of Publication: November 29, 2011

Author: The Reinvestment Fund

Overview

This chapter provides users with an overview of The Reinvestment Fund's (TRF) Limited Supermarket Access (LSA) analysis, an important new tool which helps CDFIs access robust analysis related to communities with limited access to healthy foods. The LSA was conducted as part of the Community Development Financial Institutions Fund's (CDFI Fund) Financing Healthy Food Options track, provided by Opportunity Finance Network (OFN), and is available through PolicyMap, an online data and mapping tool. Accessing the information through PolicyMap.com offers CDFIs the ability to further understand the characteristics of an LSA area by overlaying data related to income, race, age, and more.

Identifying Areas with Need for Public Intervention:

Beginning in 1990, researchers, communities and policymakers started defining areas with limited access to food retail locations as 'food deserts'. The definition of what constitutes a 'food desert' and the methods and data used to identify and characterize these areas varies greatly, resulting in diverse opinions on the extent of the problem and its location. TRF, with support from the CDFI Fund, sought to define and measure limited access: Where are households that have limited access to full service supermarkets? TRF's approach established benchmark travel distances (while accounting for the diversity of both population density and car ownership rates in the US) and used full service supermarkets[1] as a proxy for access to healthy, affordable foods. Our study of areas with Limited Supermarket Access (LSA) was designed specifically to:

(a) Prioritize underserved areas based on their level of grocery retail leakage, demand, and lack of access;

(b) Identify optimal areas for supermarket development;

(c) Display the results at various levels of geography ranging from the census block groups, to nation;

(d) Design a tool that helps a diverse range of clients, including policymakers, government agencies, businesses, foundations, financial institutions, and policy research organizations to understand Low Access Areas, and craft strategies based upon the conditions in their community.

Method for Identifying Limited Supermarket Access (LSA) areas, as of 2011:

TRF's methodology is designed to identify areas[1] where residents travel longer distances to reach a supermarket when compared to the average distance traveled by non-low/moderate income areas to access a supermarket. The areas are compared to other areas that share similar values for population density and car ownership rates.

Map 1 : Nationwide map showing Low Supermarket Access Areas

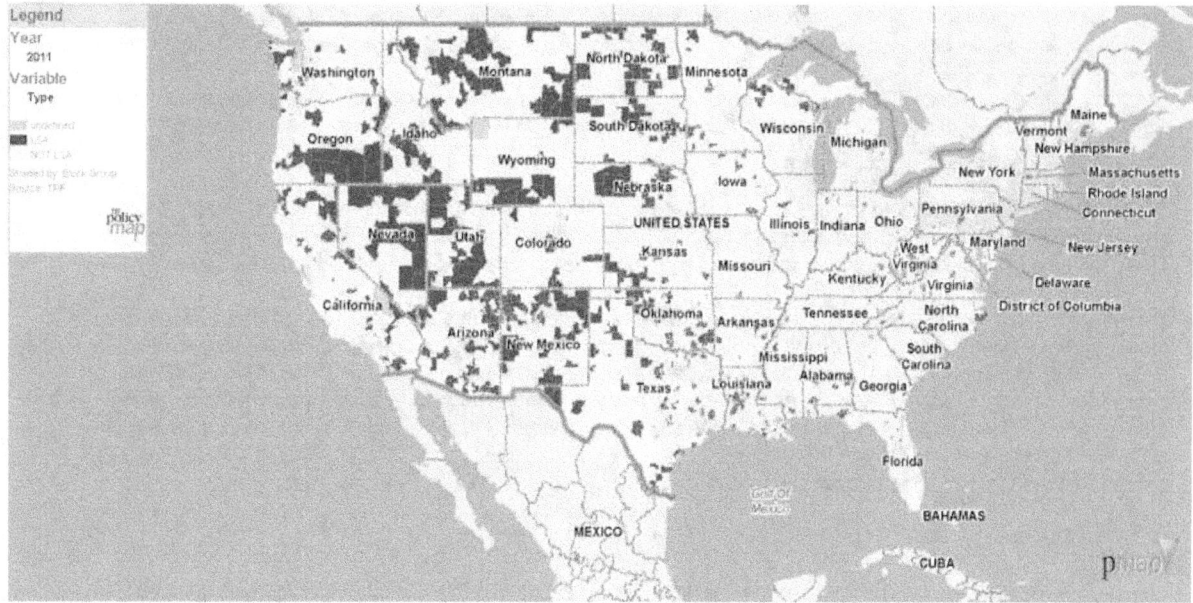

Our data sources include US Census (2010) for population living in households, residential land area, and car ownership rate; and Trade Dimensions (2011) for supermarket locations[2].

Many prior research efforts to identify underserved areas have used fixed distances for urban, suburban, and rural areas throughout entire counties, metro areas, and even states; TRF's methodology accounts for the wide-ranging values for population density and car ownership rate and their significant influence on how far households are expected to travel to shop for food. This methodology's key assumption is that block groups with a median household income greater than 120% of their respective metro area household median (or non-metro state median for non-metro areas) are adequately served by supermarkets and thus travel an appropriate distance. This assumption establishes the benchmark to which all block groups are compared. This assumption is based on existing research that indicates an intense level of competition in the supermarket industry in higher-income communities.

Step I. Classify Population Density: TRF categorized all block groups in the continental US using Census data for population density and car ownership. This process results in 13 categories ranging from "Density 1 (lowest density – high car ownership) to Density 7 (highest density – lowest car ownership). *Note that block groups with fewer than 250 people were excluded because they do not represent the typical community structure, in that a significant portion of the land area contains non-residential uses (these may include park land, largely industrial or commercial areas).*

Step II. Calculate Network Distance: TRF then calculated the distance travelled using actual roads from the population center of every census block (or block centroid) to the nearest "full-service" store. For each census block group a population-weighted distance was established based on distance traveled by each of the member blocks.

Step III. Establish Benchmarks: TRF calculated benchmark distances based on our key assumption noted above. Each benchmark represents the average block group (calculated in Step II) distance of all non-low/moderate income (LMI) block groups and their nearest supermarket, within each category created in Step I. The benchmark distance represents a comparatively acceptable distance for households to travel to a supermarket.

Step IV. Calculate Access Score: TRF calculated an access score for each block group which represents the percent that the block group distance needs to be lowered in order to reach the reference group distance. These are referred to as Access Scores.

Step V. Identify Limited Supermarket Access areas: TRF used spatial-statistical methods to identify block groups clustered together with high access scores that have neighboring block groups with high access scores. These identified areas represent spatial clusters of high low access scores and are referred to as LSA areas.

Step VI. TRF created retail grocery leakage estimates as a way to determine the magnitude of each LSA's access problem and its potential remedy – leakage represents grocery purchases made outside of the LSA boundaries. Using household income categories and their respective percentages of income spent on "food at home" (Consumer Expenditure Survey, 2011), TRF estimated total retail grocery demand in each LSA. Total grocery sales occurring within each LSA (from superettes and limited assortment stores) were then subtracted from demand, resulting in estimates for retail grocery leakage. Because the access problem is better understood in terms of square feet, TRF converted dollars leaked to square feet using nationwide weighted averages for sales per square foot.

Utilizing the Data

The designated LSAs can be analyzed and ranked using variables included in the analysis to inform local strategies and policy and engage operators. Information is available to answer questions such as: How much retail leakage is occurring?; What is the consumer demand for an area?; How does this area's access compare to well served communities?; or What is the demographic profile of this community?

Access scores and grocery leakage are two metrics which can help policymakers sort and compare LSAs. The access score describes the severity of the access in Limited Supermarket Access areas, while the leakage measure represents the estimated amount of dollars a household spends outside its area on food to prepare at home. These two measures can help policymakers match appropriate policy interventions to areas that need them the most. CDFIs and program administrators can look within a specific selected geography to compare and understand the opportunities of each LSA.

Understanding and Analyzing LSAs Using PolicyMap: Philadelphia Example

TRF's Study is available to the public through www.policymap.com. A complete copy of the study will be available on the TRF website. The PolicyMap platform allows users to view information in tabular, map and report formats as well as access the extraordinary amount of data available through PolicyMap to understand real estate markets and the communities in need of supermarket access. The following is one example using some of the available dataset to determine where the need for supermarkets may exist in the City of Philadelphia.

---

[1] "Supermarkets" include all grocery store types (supermarkets, supercenters, warehouse, limited assortment or natural foods) except "superettes" as defined by Trade Dimensions (a Nielsen Media company), because they are less likely to provide a wide range of fresh groceries.

[2] US Census block groups serve as the unit of analysis; "areas" are clusters of underserved block groups.

Map 2: Map of Philadelphia with Low Supermarket Access Area Status as of 2011

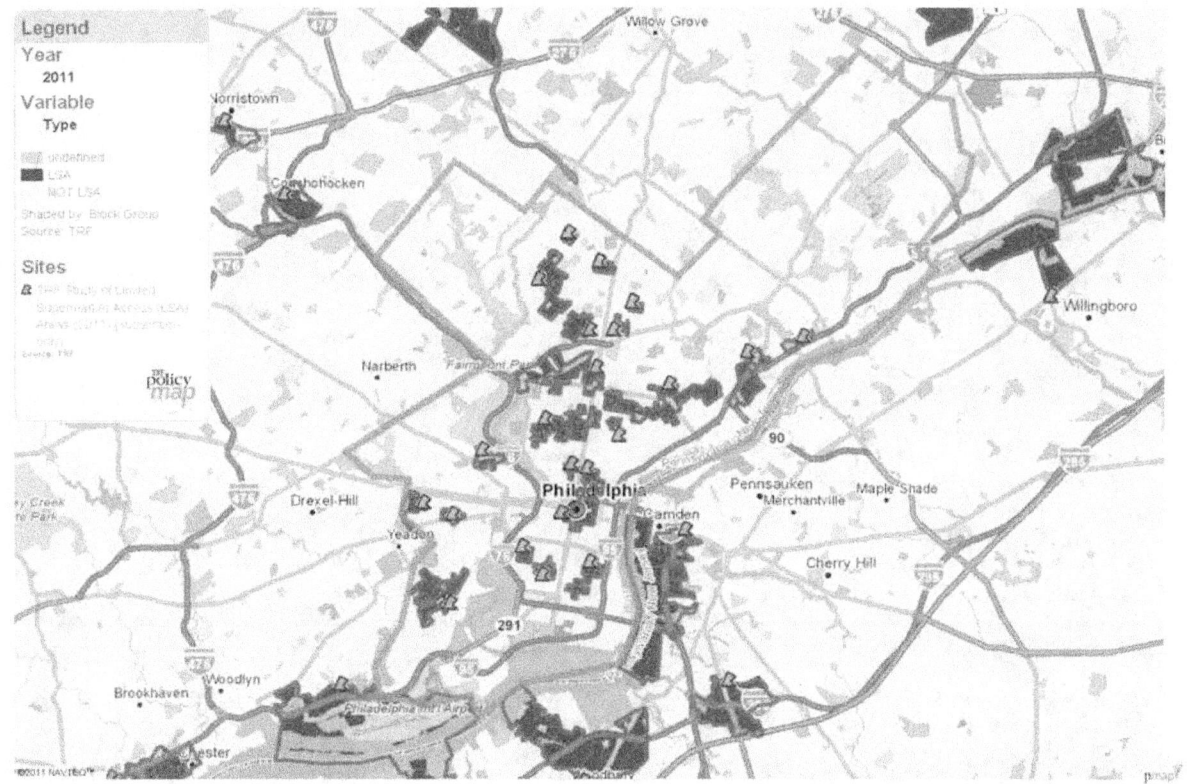

Here is a map of the City of Philadelphia (Map 2), the orange outline is the City border; in purple (outlined in blue) are the areas designated as LSA areas. Within the City there are 22 LSA areas. From the map you can either click on a specific LSA area to look at the data for that area or use the PolicyMap.com report function to export the data on all of these areas into a table.

A CDFI working in this City may have a specific geographic area where they are interested in supporting a project, or if they have a citywide agenda, may be interested in attracting a supermarket to an area of greatest need. The information provided in Table 1 below can be used to drive that discussion. In this case, if interested in identifying the LSA area with the highest leakage, you would see LSA Philadelphia County, Pennsylvania 13 is composed of 37 block groups and has an estimated leakage of $27,700,000.

Table 1: Listing of Philadelphia Low Supermarket Access Areas, PolicyMap Report

Limited Supermarket Access (LSA) Name	Population Weighted LSA Score	# Block Groups in LSA	Est. Grocery Retail Leakage Amount	Est. Grocery Retail Leakage Rate	Est. Total Grocery Retail Demand	Est. Total Grocery Retail Sq Ft Demand	Est. # Grocery Retail Sq Ft Leaked	# Limited Access Stores in LSA	Population
LSA Philadelphia County, Pennsylvania 19	50	18	18,800,000	93	20,300,000	36000	33000	5	17825
LSA Philadelphia County, Pennsylvania 8	56	13	17,800,000	80	22,200,000	39000	31000	6	17710
LSA Philadelphia County, Pennsylvania 7	58	3	2,300,000	98	2,400,000	4000	4000	1	1749
LSA Philadelphia County, Pennsylvania 9	55	5	4,500,000	86	5,200,000	9000	8000	3	4215
LSA Philadelphia County, Pennsylvania 12	54	5	4,700,000	95	5,000,000	9000	8000	0	3999
LSA Philadelphia County, Pennsylvania 14	54	6	8,100,000	93	8,700,000	15000	14000	1	6484
LSA Philadelphia County, Pennsylvania 18	51	18	27,200,000	78	34,800,000	61000	48000	16	19094
LSA Philadelphia County, Pennsylvania 1	69	7	3,400,000	81	4,100,000	7000	6000	2	3830
LSA Philadelphia County, Pennsylvania 22	48	5	1,900,000	76	2,500,000	4000	3000	1	2137
LSA Philadelphia County, Pennsylvania 17	52	9	6,800,000	79	8,600,000	15000	12000	2	6162
LSA Philadelphia County, Pennsylvania 4	60	5	2,300,000	100	2,300,000	4000	4000	0	2379
LSA Philadelphia County, Pennsylvania 15	53	4	2,600,000	69	3,700,000	7000	5000	1	3472
LSA Philadelphia County, Pennsylvania 10	55	8	6,700,000	88	7,700,000	13000	12000	2	5781
LSA Philadelphia County, Pennsylvania 2	66	2	2,100,000	99	2,100,000	4000	4000	0	1738
LSA Philadelphia County, Pennsylvania 11	55	4	5,000,000	87	5,800,000	10000	9000	0	3614
LSA Philadelphia County, Pennsylvania 6	59	2	1,400,000	97	1,400,000	3000	2000	1	831
LSA Philadelphia County, Pennsylvania 21	48	14	13,100,000	84	15,500,000	27000	23000	6	11574
LSA Philadelphia County, Pennsylvania 16	53	8	9,200,000	82	11,200,000	20000	16000	3	9224
LSA Philadelphia County, Pennsylvania 5	60	31	21,000,000	80	26,300,000	46000	37000	6	24321
LSA Philadelphia County, Pennsylvania 13	54	37	27,700,000	77	35,800,000	63000	49000	12	38288
LSA Philadelphia County, Pennsylvania 3	62	23	22,000,000	93	23,700,000	42000	39000	4	17091
LSA Philadelphia County, Pennsylvania 20	48	15	14,700,000	94	15,700,000	27000	26000	3	12209

You can then use the PolicyMap.com search function to find polygon "LSA Philadelphia County, Pennsylvania 13" and view the opportunity and market conditions within the specific area or run a Community Profile Report for that area or a subset of that area. Map 3 below shows the specific LSA:

Map 3: Map of Philadelphia showing grocery retail locations and Low Supermarket Access Area status as of 2011

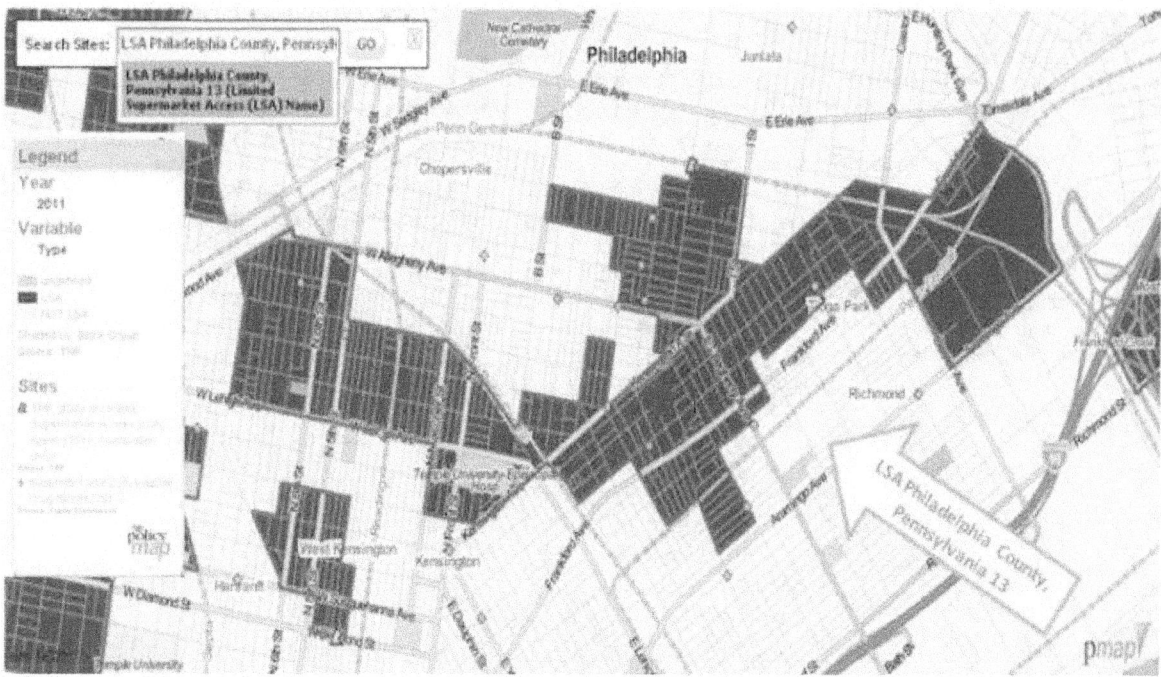

Map 3 also shows all store locations within LSA 13. An LSA area will not have full service supermarkets within their boundaries, but they may have other food retail locations. In this case, there are 12 superettes. The leakage number is also converted for the user into square feet. An area of this size appears to be able to support 1 full service supermarket. In order to determine if and where a store may be feasible and how it may impact existing stores operating in other parts of the city, a user may want to also consider:

- *Where are the supermarkets located outside of the area?;*
- *What is the quality of the superettes within the area?; and*
- *What is the market profile of the community?*

(Note: Implementation Handbook chapter titled *Understanding the Grocery Industry* provides definitions of grocery industry formats, including superettes and full-serve supermarkets).

LSA Philadelphia County, Pennsylvania 13 covers a large area. A user may also want to divide the area into smaller segments based upon known natural boundaries between neighborhoods or demographic information about the communities. Users can create custom regions on top of the LSA area to determine where to locate a store to meet

the greatest need and look at the data for these specific areas. Many demorgaphic data sets are available through PolicyMap.

Information including population trends, racial characteristics, age and incomes of households can be gathered from PolicyMap's Community Profile Report. From this report, users can gather that as of 2009, this area was home to an estimated 37,782 people. In the report area from 2005-2009, 5.84% of the population is over the age of 65. 54.69% are of working age (18-64). 39.47% are under 18, and 11.54% are under 5 years old. During the same period, 30.38% of the area's population was white, 30.67% was African American, 2.12% was Asian, 0.28% was American Indian or Alaskan Native, and 57.14% identified as Hispanic. In 2009, 86.62%% of households in the study area had an annual income of less than $50,000, compared to 50.24% of people in Pennsylvania. The Community Profile Report also identified the state and federal elected officials representing this area.

The data can be viewed at even more specific levels of geography to locate the households with the highest level of poverty or the areas that have the most diverse income levels. Operators may be drawn to areas that have the potential to serve a wider range of income levels. They may operate a range of store types, some that are more viable in low-income communities. Viewing demographic data can inform that conversation. Demographic data can also offer an understanding of what is required to make a store attractive to the community. For example, an operator locating in a high density low-income community will likely need to secure a WIC and/or SNAP certification before openning a store. While this will not replace a market study required by most financial institutions, it will report many of the variables a store's marketing department gathers when evaluating a site. This data is also useful for CDFIs to view when evaluating potential requests for financing as a means to validate the borrower's pro forma and overall project.

PolicyMap also provides some point level data that can be added to maps as well. Map 4, shows the *Estimated percent of families that live in Poverty,* and the location of public transit stops. This can be used to understand which of the possible sites is located closest to transit stops *(some public financing programs provide applicants with additional points to projects that are in transit areas)* and it may assist a project to maximize convienence for shoppers already in transit and for those with limited access to a car.

Map 4: Map showing estimated percentage of all families that live in poverty between 2005 – 2009.

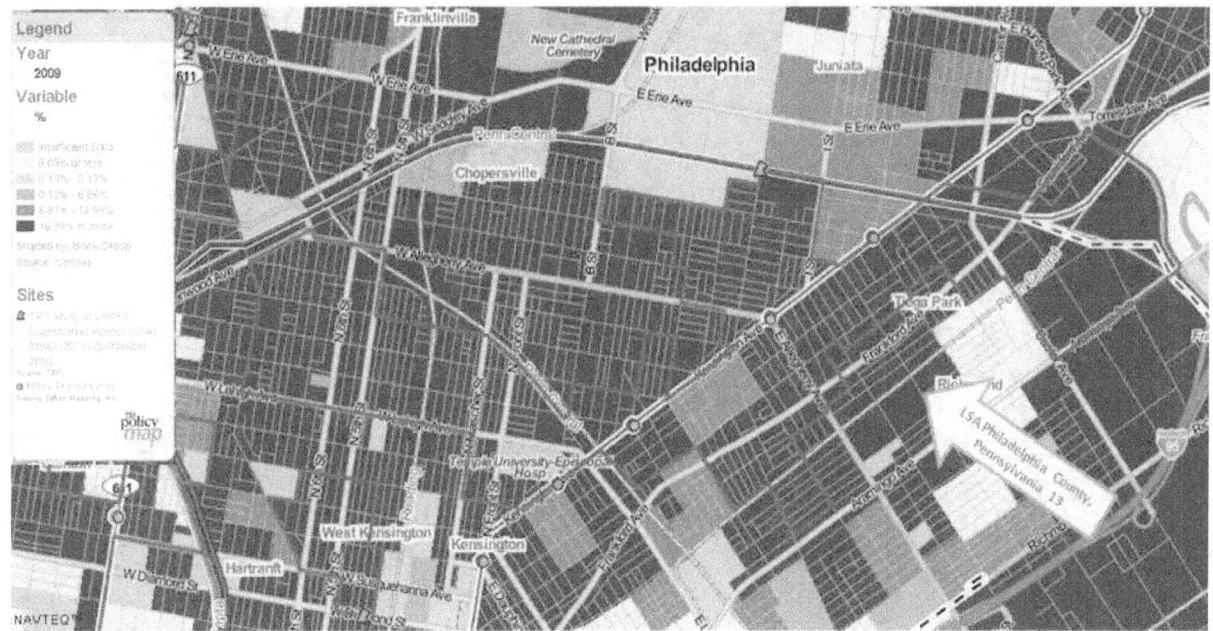

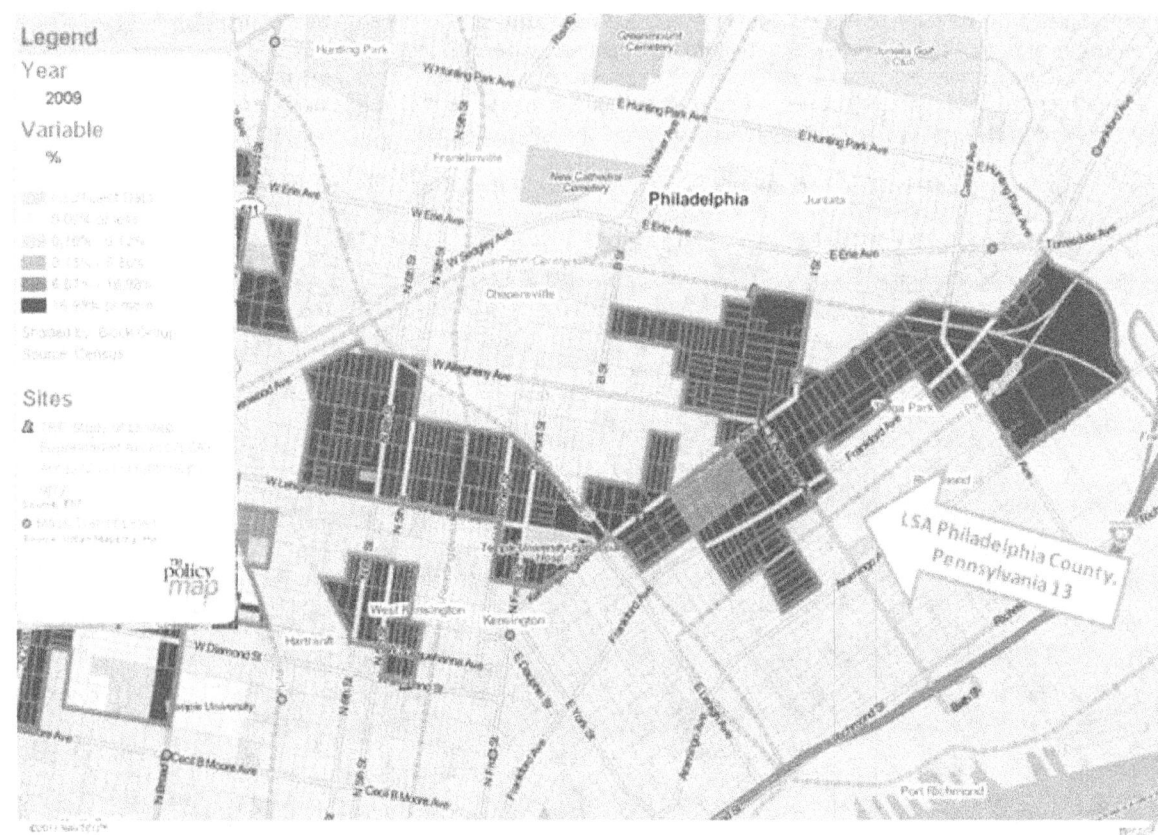

In trying to match areas with need with areas that provide economic incentives to operators and developers, it is also useful to view the areas that are eligible for economic and community development incentives. For example, Map 5 shows LSA areas that meet the *CDFI Fund's NMTC Program criteria for severly distressed*. Only the areas that meet both criteria are shaded. PolicyMap has many federal programs in the data warehouse, including the USDA Food Desert Study and Community Development Block Grant (CDBG) eligible tracts. Users can map both the TRF LSA polygons (shapes) and the federal program guidelines (thematic colored layers) at the same time to find optimal locations for both meeting need and accessing resources.

Map 5: This map shows the NMTC program's severe distress status against Low Supermarket Access Area status. Areas within the blue boundaries meet both criteria.

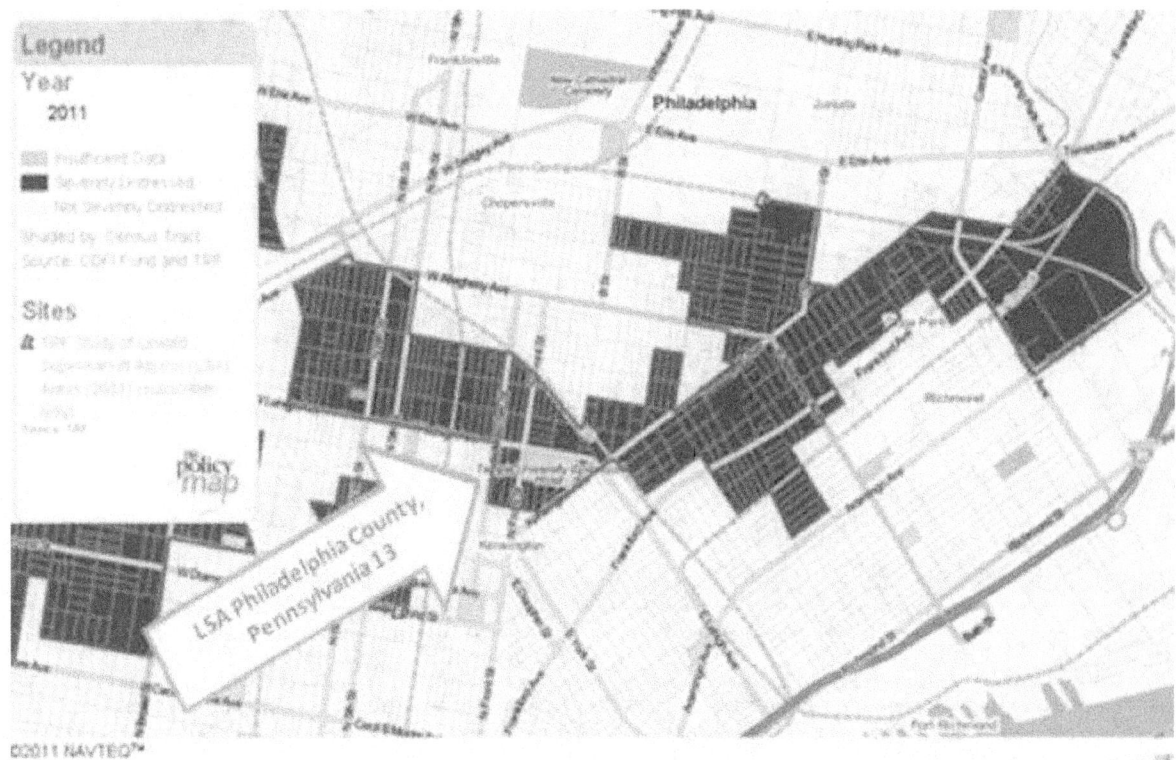

PolicyMap provides users with many ways to rank or prioritize the areas. If a specific site is under consideration, users can create a radius and run a **Community Profile Report** from that address. Map 6 shows what this would look like. All maps can be saved, shared and printed to increase collaboration and communication about areas' needs and opportunities with the policymakers and local partners.

Map 6: Map of LSA Philadelphia County, Pennsylvania 13 showing 0.5 mile radius.

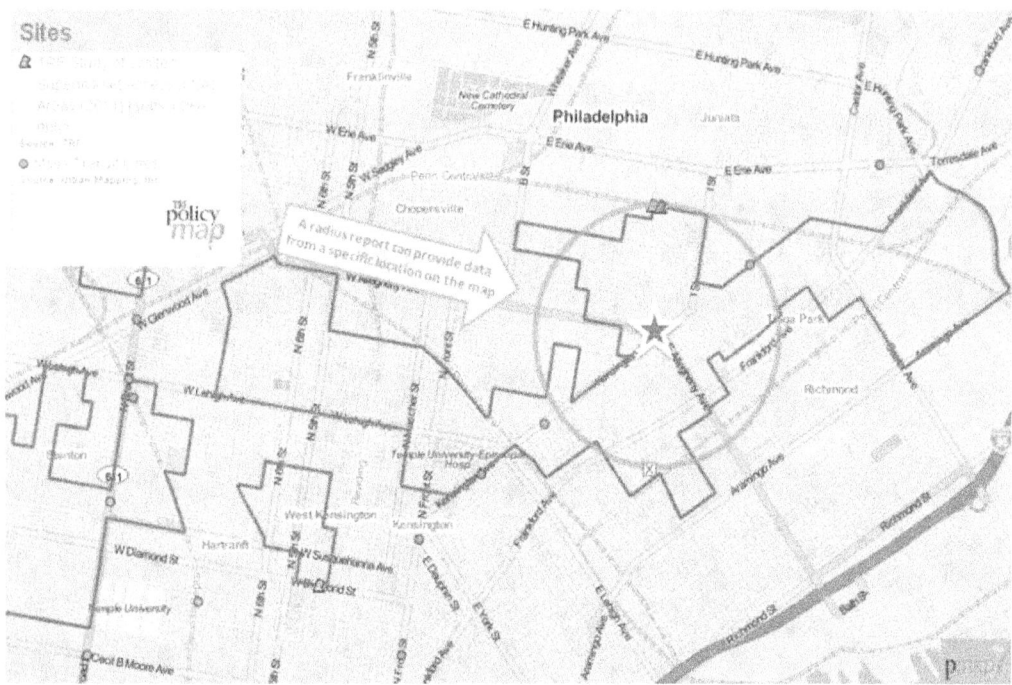

This Philadelphia example shows the analytic tool working from a metro area to a specific site. The same process could be followed to look at results at a statewide or county level and then drilled down to a specific LSA area, or to look at how a specific area compares to other areas in the City and State.

Just as an operator or developer will send staff to assess sites, entities working with the data still need to visit a location to validate and understand the specific opportunities and challenges presented within a geographic area. This is point in time data that is updated on an annual basis, so if a new store opens or an existing store closes after the TRF analysis is complete it will not be shown until the data is updated. Site visits also offer an opportunity to collect additional data. This primary data can be uploaded, displayed, and shared with others on PolicyMap. For Example: A user may conduct physical surveys of the area and observe: where are possible sites to locate a store; where is the land zoned for this commercial use; and/or where are there housing development sites under construction. This address level data can be loaded directly onto PolicyMap by the subscriber, or a Premium Subscriber can submit this data to PolicyMap staff and have the information loaded into PolicyMap for them.

Research conducted by Policy Solutions at The Reinvestment Fund
Catherine Califano, Associate Director
Kennen Gross, Senior Research Associate
Lance Loethen, Research Associate
Scott Haag, GIS and Database Manager
Ira Goldstein, Director

Special thanks to research assistance provided by:
Kavita Vijayan, Lee West, Wing Lock Li, and Annie Tickell

Graphic Design: Morgan Johnson

Copy Editor: Janet Benton, The Word Studio

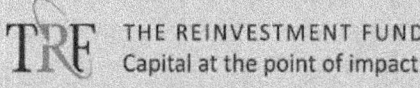

THE REINVESTMENT FUND
Capital at the point of impact.

OPPORTUNITYFINANCE
NETWORK